An integrated course for communicative success

Wanna Talk

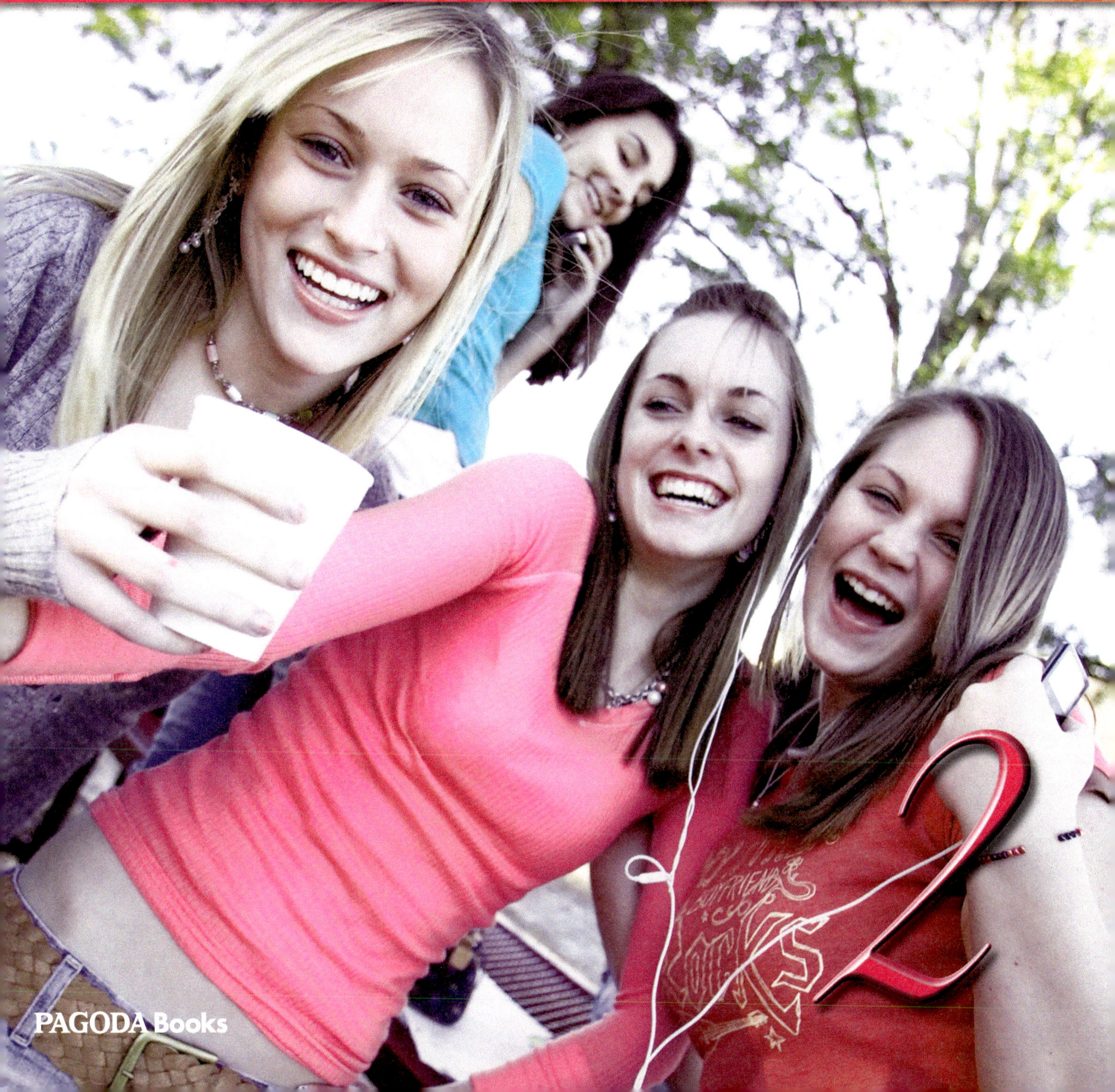

2

PAGODA Books

INTRODUCTION

Wanna Talk 2 is the second book in the **Wanna Talk** series, a three-level course specially designed for beginning through intermediate level students who are studying English as a foreign language. **Wanna Talk 2** gives students more opportunities than other books of its kind to learn English through a diversity of activities. The course combines listening, speaking, reading and writing activities. Students are able to actively participate in meaningful exchanges during pair work and group work. The primary goal of the course is to help students communicate appropriately and effectively according to the situation, purpose and roles of the participants. It is designed to promote language acquisition through student participation in purposeful interaction. Each unit in this book revolves around a practical theme and contains the following sections.

Get started

This section introduces the principal topic of the unit and stimulates students' interest in the theme of the unit. It presents the unit's frequently used vocabulary and language points in diverse ways.

Talk together

In this section, students will listen to a dialogue and then practice with a partner. The dialogue employs everyday language in a wide range of real-life settings and situations. This section also includes the main language expressions of the unit.

Language focus

This section contains an overview of the sentence structures and key expressions presented in the unit. This provides language models for the students that they can use as a quick reference while doing the exercises.

Practice more

This section provides more opportunities for the students to do drill exercises using the key expressions from the *Language focus* section.

Let's do it 1 & 2

These two sections contain both listening and speaking activities. Students can practice more conversational functions and strategies based on the key expressions and topic of the unit. It aims to build students' confidence in communicative situations. Moreover, pair work and group work activities help students expand on what they have learned and to use the language for more meaningful and freer speaking practice.

CONTENTS

- Introduction — 2
- Scope and Sequence — 4

- **UNIT 01** How are you doing? — 7
- **UNIT 02** What date is your birthday? — 15
- **UNIT 03** What's the weather like? — 23
- **UNIT 04** What does it look like? — 31
- **UNIT 05** Do you have any plans for the weekend? — 39
- **UNIT 06** What kind of dress are you looking for? — 47
- **UNIT 07** What do you think of jazz? — 55
- **UNIT 08** What would you like to have? — 63
- **UNIT 09** Are you under the weather? — 71
- **UNIT 10** What is your place like? — 79
- **UNIT 11** Who does he work for? — 87
- **UNIT 12** Could you ask him to call me back? — 95

- Listening Script — 103

Reading
The *Reading* section exposes students to a wide variety of authentic and topic related content. Therefore, students can expand their real life knowledge and develop their ability to use that knowledge in the topic related communication. This section also helps students develop critical thinking skills and inferencing skills.

Writing
The *Writing* section helps students to enhance their writing skills with a variety of short writing tasks. It enables students to relate what they have learned in the unit with their personal experiences through meaningful writing practice. Students are therefore given the chance to express themselves in writing as well as practice newly acquired structures and vocabulary.

SCOPE AND SEQUENCE

Unit	Topics	Functions	Grammar
01 How are you doing?	• Introductions • Greetings • Nationalities • Occupations • Personal information	• Greeting each other • Introducing yourself and others • Making a proper introduction • Asking for and answering personal information • Talking about personal ads from a newspaper	• Simple present: *Wh-* questions and statements
02 What date is your birthday?	• Times of the day • Days of the week • Dates • Months • Holidays and special occasions	• Asking for and telling the time • Talking about days and dates • Talking about starting/ending, opening/closing times • Talking about the dates of special days or holidays • Talking about what people do on special days in different countries	• The verb *Be*: *Wh-* questions and statements • Simple present: *Wh-* questions and statements • Prepositions in time expressions: *at/on/in* • Future tense with *be going to*
03 What's the weather like?	• Weather conditions • Temperature • Seasonal climates • Seasonal activities	• Describing weather conditions • Talking about temperatures • Talking about one's favorite weather and seasons • Talking about activities based on weather conditions and seasons	• Adjectives for describing weather conditions • The verb *Be*: *Wh-* questions and statements • Simple present: *Wh-* questions and statements
04 What does it look like?	• Describing things • Names of objects • Features of objects • Uses of objects • Comparing things • Preferences	• Describing shapes, colors, and materials of objects • Describing features of objects • Talking about uses of objects • Making comparisons • Asking and talking about preferences	• Adjectives for describing shapes and colors • Comparative and superlative forms of adjectives • The verb *Be*: *Wh-* questions with comparatives • Simple present: *Wh-* questions and statements with comparatives

Unit	Topics	Functions	Grammar
05 Do you have any plans for the weekend?	• Weekend plans • Vacations • Future plans • Hopes and resolutions • Future dreams	• Talking about weekend plans • Planning a vacation • Talking about schedules and future plans • Talking about hopes, dreams, and resolutions	• Future tense with *be going to* and *be + ing* • Simple present for future • *What would you like to...?*
06 What kind of dress are you looking for?	• Shopping • Names, sizes, features, colors of objects • Different store types and sales • Describing problems with items • Exchanging, returning, and refunding	• Buying and selling things • Asking and answering information about features of objects • Exchanging and returning things; getting a refund • Describing problems with objects	• The verb *Be*: *Wh-* questions and statements • Simple present: *Yes/No* questions and short answers
07 What do you think of jazz?	• Favorites • Likes and dislikes • Free time activities	• Talking about likes and dislikes • Talking about free time activities • Asking for and giving opinions • Talking about favorite types of entertainment	• Simple present: *Yes/No* questions and *Wh-* questions • *What kind of...?*
08 What would you like to have?	• Food and drink • Meals • Recipes • Restaurants	• Reading a menu • Ordering meals • Giving and taking orders in a restaurant • Checking on customers • Giving cooking instructions	• *Would you like* + noun...? • *What would you like to...?* • Imperatives

SCOPE AND SEQUENCE

Unit	Topics	Functions	Grammar
09 Are you under the weather?	• Illness • Remedies • Appointments	• Talking about health problems • Describing symptoms • Naming specialists • Making appointments with a doctor • Giving advice and suggestions about health problems	• Simple present • *You should*+verb... • *Why don't you...?*
10 What is your place like?	• House • Apartment • Rooms • Real estate	• Talking about different types of housing • Describing homes; areas, rooms, and features • Calling about an apartment or a house for rent • Reporting housing problems • Talking about a dream house	• Simple present: *Yes/No* questions and *Wh-* questions • The verb *Be*: *Yes/No* questions and *Wh-* questions • *How many...are there?* • *There is.../There are...* • Prepositions of place
11 Who does he work for?	• Occupations • Workplaces • Job advertisements • Qualifications	• Talking about occupations and workplaces • Talking about how people like their job and giving opinions about work • Asking for and giving information about work • Talking about skills and qualities needed for jobs • Reading job advertisements	• Simple present: *Wh-* questions and statements • Descriptive adjectives for occupations
12 Could you ask him to call me back?	• Communication • Phone calls • Keeping in touch	• Talking about different ways people communicate • Comparing ways of keeping in touch • Managing phone conversations • Talking about advantages and disadvantages of different communication methods	• Simple present • *Can I...?/May I...?* • *Could you...?* • Imperatives with *please* • *Ask/Tell*+someone+*to do*

01 How are you doing?

Lesson Focus

- 01 Greetings
- 02 Introducing themselves and others
- 03 Making polite conversation
- 04 Using *wh*-questions in relation to personal information exchanges

UNIT 01 How are you doing?

Get started

A. Anita just finished filling out a job application form. With the information on the form, complete the questions on the right. Then take turns asking and answering the questions with your partner.

Application

1 Last name	Fuller
2 First name	Anita
3 Address	209 Beach Avenue, Vancouver, British Columbia
4 Phone number	(604) 606-7224
5 Occupation	French teacher
6 E-mail address	anita_07@gmail.com
7 Date of birth	Jan 13, 1977
8 Marital status	Single
9 Nationality	Canadian

Questions

1. What's her ....?
2. What's her ....?
3. .... does she live?
4. .... her .... number?
5. What .... she do?
6. What's her ....?
7. When .... she born?
8. Is she .... or ....?
9. What's her ....?

B. Pair work. Ask your partner for his/her personal information using the questions in Part **A**. Then fill out the form below with your partner's answers.

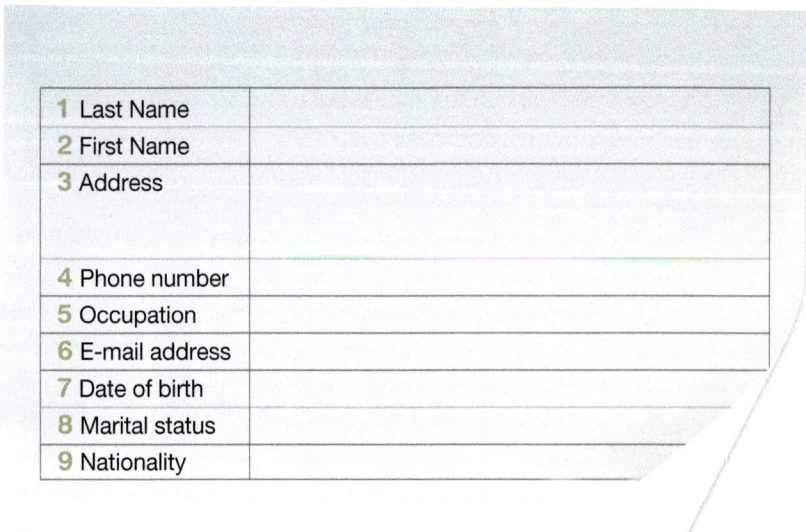

1 Last Name	
2 First Name	
3 Address	
4 Phone number	
5 Occupation	
6 E-mail address	
7 Date of birth	
8 Marital status	
9 Nationality	

Talk together 🎧

Listen to the dialogue and practice.

Robert: Hi, Emily! How's it going?
Emily: Not bad. And you?
Robert: Pretty good. Actually, I am very busy with a presentation.
Emily: I see. By the way, I'd like you to meet my classmate, Joan. She's from Australia. Joan, this is my friend, Robert. He's from England.
Robert: Glad to meet you, Joan. Just call me Bob.
Joan: It's nice to meet you, too, Bob.
Robert: How do you know each other?
Emily: Well, Joan is an exchange student, and we are roommates.
Robert: Oh, I see. So what school do you go to?
Joan: Brisbane College.
Robert: That's nice. Anyway, let's get together some time, okay?
Emily: Sure. Take care. Bye!

Language focus

Greetings	Responses
Nice to meet you. Glad to meet you.	Nice to meet you, too. Glad to meet you, too.
Robert, let me introduce you to my friend, Joan. Joan, I'd like you to meet my friend, Robert.	Nice to meet you, Robert. I'm Joan. Glad to meet you, Joan. Just call me Bob.
How are you? (How are you doing?) How's it going? (How are things going?)	Great. / Pretty good. / Fine, thanks. / OK. Not bad. / So-so. / Terrible.
What's up? What's new?	Not much. Nothing much. I'm busy with work.
What do you do?	I'm an accountant.
What do you like to do in your free time?	I like to go for a walk.

Practice more

A. People are introducing each other at a party. With your partner, make dialogues using the information given. Follow the example.

> **Example**
>
> **Anne:** Hello, Ryan.
>
> **Ryan:** Hi, Anne. How are you doing?
>
> **Anne:** Great. By the way, I'd like you to meet my friend, Daniel. He's from England. Daniel, this is Ryan.
>
> **Daniel:** Nice to meet you, Ryan. You can call me Dan.
>
> **Ryan:** Glad to meet you, too, Dan.

Pamela - Pam	Matthew - Matt	Alexander - Alex	Patricia - Pat
Scotland	Hawaii	India	Alaska

Elizabeth - Liz	Jonathan - Jon	Daniel - Dan	William - Bill
Greece	Canada	Hong Kong	New Zealand

B. Work in pairs. Practice the dialogue below using the information given.

> **Jasmine:** Hi, I'm Jasmine from the Philippines.
>
> **Simon:** Hi, I'm Simon from Wales.
>
> **Jasmine:** What do you do?
>
> **Simon:** I work as a sales manager. What about you?
>
> **Jasmine:** I'm a nurse. So what do you like to do in your free time?
>
> **Simon:** I like watching football games.
>
> **Jasmine:** That's nice. I like playing tennis.

Brian
- China
- librarian
- traveling

Ellen
- Australia
- web designer
- cooking

Frank
- Poland
- police officer
- going hiking

Cindy
- Singapore
- accountant
- playing the violin

Let's do it 1

A. Listen to people introducing each other. They are asking and answering the questions listed below. Complete the answers based on the conversations.

	Conversation 1	Conversation 2
Questions	**Answers**	**Answers**
What's your name?	I am	I am
What do you do?	I'm a / an	I'm
Where do you work? (What school do you go to?)	I work for	I go to
Do you have any brothers or sisters?	Yes. I have and	No. I'm an
What do you like to do for fun?	I like	I like
Why do you study English?	Because I often go on abroad.	Because I want to with people from other countries.

B. Using the questions above, interview three classmates. Fill in the charts with the information you find out about your classmates.

Classmate 1	Classmate 2	Classmate 3
Name:	Name:	Name:
Job:	Job:	Job:
Workplace/School:	Workplace/School:	Workplace/School:
Siblings:	Siblings:	Siblings:
Pastime activities:	Pastime activities:	Pastime activities:
Reason for studying English:	Reason for studying English:	Reason for studying English:

C. Present the information you gathered about one of the classmates to the class.

Example

I'd like to introduce my classmate, Peter Wilson. He is an accountant and he works for Ace Bank. He has two younger sisters and one older brother. Peter likes swimming and jogging. He studies English because he really enjoys talking with people from other countries.

Let's do it 2

A. In the coffee lounge of a trading company, new employees from different departments are talking together. Listen to their conversations and fill in the table.

Conversation 1	What they do	How they get to work	Things they usually do after work
Andy			
Pam			

Conversation 2	What they do	How they get to work	Things they usually do after work
Karen			
Danny			

B. Imagine you and your partner have just met at the training session for new employees. Introduce yourselves, talk about what you do at the company, and what you like to do after work. Follow the example below. Use the information in the tables in Part **A**. Then use your own information.

> A: Hello, I'm Jenny. Nice to meet you.
> B: Hi, I'm Eddy. Glad to meet you, too.
> A: Which department do you work in?
> B: I work in the Human Resources department. What about you?
> A: I work for the Accounting department. What do you do in your department?
> B: I hire people. And you? What exactly do you do there?
> A: I work as a bookkeeper. By the way, what do you like to do after work?
> B: I usually go home, make dinner, and then take my dog for a walk. How about you?
> A: I always go to the gym and work out. Sometimes I go running in the park.

Reading

A. These are ads in the personal section of a newspaper. What are the ads about?

Looking for a friend

I'm 26, female, & a graphic designer, looking for language/cultural exchange.
I love theater/film acting and reading English books by C. S. Lewis.
I would like to keep an e-pal friendship with an English speaking person.
Please contact me at jspark@ucs.ac.uk

Interested in the arts?

I'm a 22-year-old American guy.
I'm looking for a friend who can share my passion for the arts. I'm an architect. I love music, plays, photography, and anything about art.
I just love meeting new people and would like to be friends with some folks. If you're interested in talking about the arts, please e-mail me at artistic@kmail.com

B. Answer the questions below with your partner.

1. What kind of friend is the woman in the first ad looking for?
2. What does she like to do?
3. In the second ad, what does the man do?
4. What is he interested in?

C. Imagine you'd like to place a personal ad like the ones in Part **A**. Make an outline of what you'd like to say in the ad.

Age:
Job:
E-mail:
Interests:
Purpose of the ad:

Writing

A. An e-pal is an Internet pen-pal. Read Becky's e-mail to her e-pal. What did she write about herself in the e-mail?

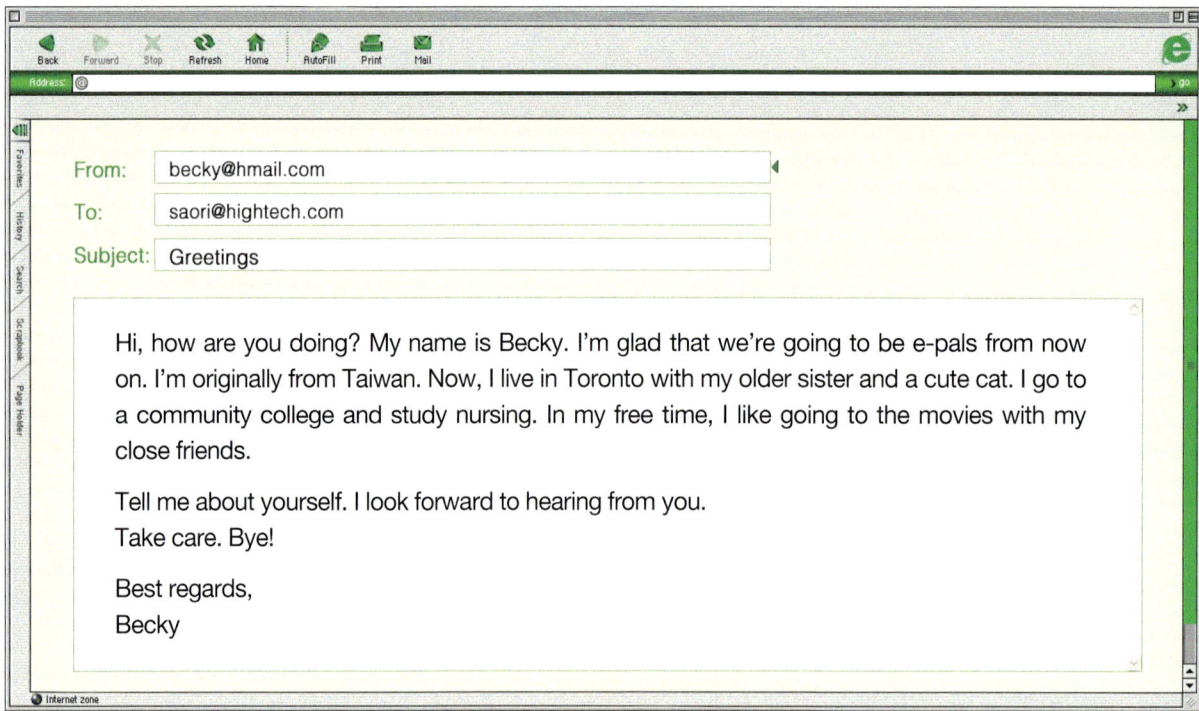

B. Pretend that you are Becky's e-pal. Write a reply to introduce yourself.

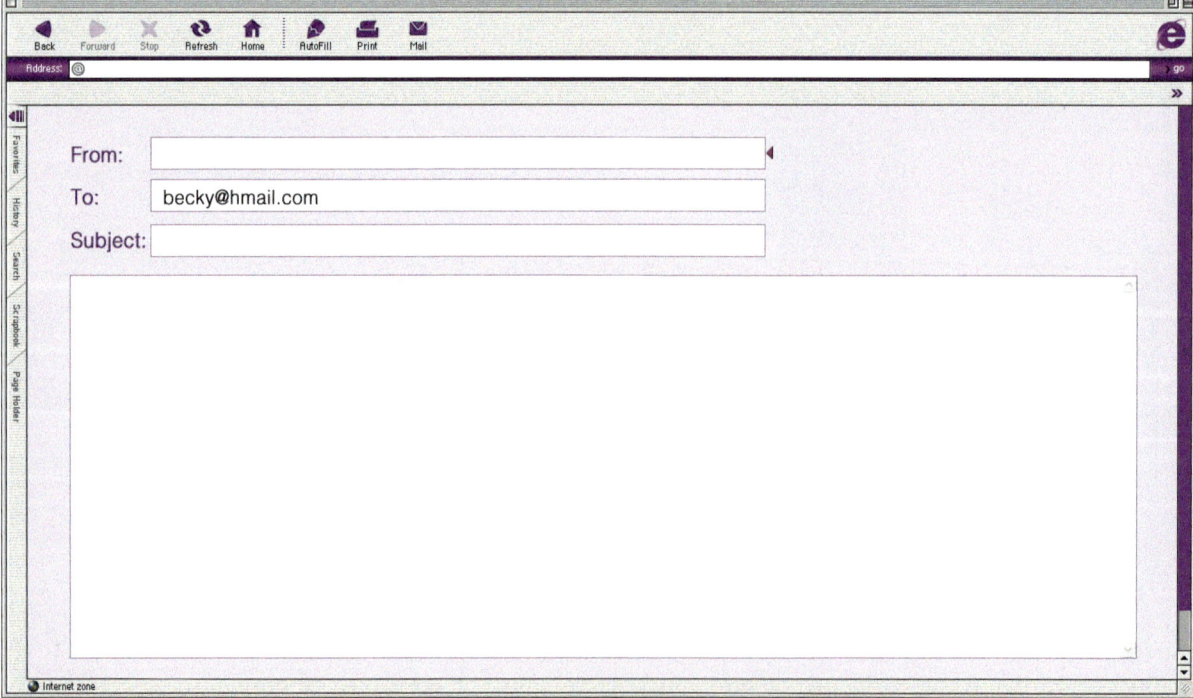

02 What date is your birthday?

Lesson Focus

01 Asking for and telling the time
02 Talking about various dates and times
03 Discussing special occasions and holidays
04 Using *wh*- questions to talk about special events and plans

UNIT 02 What date is your birthday?

Get started

A-❶. There are different kinds of holidays and special days around the world. Check the holidays or special days people celebrate in your country. Then write the dates for each.

- ☐ Valentine's Day   (2/14) the fourteenth of February
- ☐ Children's Day
- ☐ Parents' Day
- ☐ Mother's Day
- ☐ Labor Day
- ☐ Memorial Day
- ☐ Independence Day
- ☐ Thanksgiving Day
- ☐ Christmas Day
- ☐ New Year's Day

A-❷. Answer the questions with your classmates.

ⓐ Are there any holidays or special days people celebrate in your country that are not listed above? What days are they? What are the dates?
ⓑ What is your favorite holiday or special day?
ⓒ How do people celebrate your favorite holiday or special day in your country?

B. Write out the times by filling in the blanks.

It's 7 o'clock (sharp).

It's nine forty-five.
It's a _____ to ten.

It's three-thirty.
It's _____ past three.

It's ten twenty.
It's twenty _____ ten.

Talk together 🎧

Listen to the dialogue and practice.

Helen: Hey, Gina! Do you know that Claire's birthday is coming up?
Gina: Really? What date is it?
Helen: It's the 20th.
Gina: Okay. What day is that? Is it Friday?
Helen: No, it's Saturday. I am planning a surprise party for her. Would you help me out?
Gina: Sure. What do you want me to do?
Helen: Could you buy the decorations and snacks? I will bake the cake.
Gina: Okay. And what time is the party?
Helen: It's at 2:30 at my place. I was thinking we could go see "World Treasure" later on in the evening.
Gina: Great. What time does the movie start?
Helen: It starts at 9:00 p.m.
Gina: Wonderful. Sounds like a good plan.

Language focus

What time is it? Could you tell me the time? Do you have the time?	It's 7:30. (seven-thirty) It's half past seven.
What day is it today?	It's Monday.
What date is it today? What's today's date? What is the date today?	It's the 20th of December. It's December (the) 20th.
What time does the movie start (finish)? What time does the bank open (close)?	It starts (finishes) at 9 p.m. It opens at 9:30. / It closes at 5.

What date is your birthday? • 17

Practice more

A. Practice asking for and saying the different times below. Try to use *past*, *to*, *half*, and *quarter* when saying the times.

Example

A: What time is it? (Do you have the time?) → B: It's *one fifteen*. (It's *a quarter past one*.)

B. Practice asking for and saying each date.

  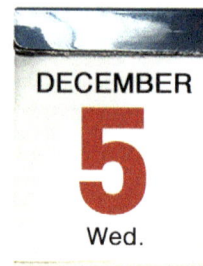  

Example

A: What day is it today? → B: It's Wednesday.
A: What date is it? → B: It's January (the) 5th.

C. Using the information in the table, talk about starting (opening) and finishing (closing) times.

	start / open	finish / close
concert	7:30 P.M.	9:30 P.M.
party	6:00 P.M.	9:00 P.M.
soccer game	8:00 P.M.	9:30 P.M.
library	9:00 A.M.	6:00 P.M.
supermarket	9:30 A.M.	12:00 A.M.

D. Write the proper preposition for each word or phrase in the blank. Use *on*, *in*, or *at*.

ⓐ .... Tuesday   ⓑ .... May   ⓒ 2006   ⓓ .... 3:30 a.m.   ⓔ .... the afternoon
ⓕ .... midnight   ⓖ .... May 5th   ⓗ .... the evening   ⓘ .... Valentine's Day

18 • UNIT 02

Let's do it 1

A-❶. Listen to two dialogues. Fill in the blanks with the correct time.

A-❷. Imagine you are going to order a special bouquet for your parents' wedding anniversary. With your partner role-play a telephone conversation between a florist and a customer about the flower shop's business hours. Use the listening scripts from **A-❶** as a guide.

A:
B:
A:
B:
A:
B:

B-❶. Listen to two dialogues and fill in the blanks with the correct time and dates.

B-❷. Role-play making plans to go to a baseball game with your partner. Discuss the date and time of the game. Use the listening scripts from **B-❶** as a guide.

Let's do it 2

A. Listen to Rachel's plans for February. Fill in the blanks in the calendar with the correct event.

- Anna's wedding
- my birthday party
- high school reunion
- dental appointment
- see a movie

02 February

SUN.	MON.	TUE.	WED.	THU.	FRI.	SAT.
				1	2 Dinner with coworkers	3
4	5	6	7	8	9	10
11	12	13	14	15	16	17
18	19	20	21	22	23	24
25	26	27	28			

B. Listen again and complete the sentences below with the activities she's going to do on the occasions.

Dates	Activities
Feb.	_____ at a Chinese restaurant with my family at _____
Feb.	See _____ at _____
Feb.	See a movie with my _____ at _____
Feb.	Go to my high school _____ at the Sheraton Hotel at _____
Feb.	Go to Anna's _____ at _____

C. Work in pairs. Talk about the plans Rachel has for February. Follow the example below.

A: When date is Rachel's birthday?
B: It's Thursday, February 8th.
A: What is she going to do?
B: She is going to eat out at a Chinese restaurant with her family.

20 • UNIT 02

Reading

A. How do people celebrate New Year's Eve in your country? Read about how people in Australia, the UK and Spain celebrate New Year's.

New Year's Eve Celebration

In Sydney, Australia, over 80,000 fireworks are traditionally set off from five firing points including the Sydney Harbour Bridge. Every year, this event attracts an average of 300,000 tourists from all over the world. The Harbour of Lights Parade is also a good attraction where boats, covered with fairy lights, cruise the harbor all night. Sydney is well-known for having one of the world's best New Year's Eve celebrations.

The English celebrate New Year's Eve by waiting for either Big Ben or another clock to strike midnight while enjoying a party. People countdown the last ten seconds by shouting out the numbers. And when Big Ben chimes at midnight, they shout "Happy New Year!" The chimes are usually accompanied by fireworks.

In Spain, people begin New Year's Eve celebrations with a family dinner which traditionally includes shrimp, lamb or turkey. It is traditional to eat 12 grapes while the clock on top of the Casa de Correos building in Puerta del Sol square in Madrid chimes for the new year. After the clock has finished striking twelve, people greet each other and toast one another with wine, champagne, or cider.

B. Answer the following questions with your partner.

1. What is the New Year's Eve celebration in Sydney like?
2. How do people celebrate New Year's Eve in London?
3. What do people usually do on New Year's Eve in Spain?
4. How about in your country? What do people do on New Year's Eve?

Writing

A. With your partner, take turns asking and answering the questions below. Complete the chart with your partner's answers.

1. What is your favorite holiday or special day?
2. What date is it?
3. What do you do on that day?
4. What kind of special food do you eat?

B. What do people in your country do on New Year's Day, Valentine's Day, or Christmas Day? Choose one of those days and write about how people celebrate it. Use the words given below.

Example

On Valentine's Day, people send their loved ones flowers or gifts. People usually send red roses, tulips, lilies, or carnations. People also buy chocolates, put them in heart-shaped boxes, and give them to their loved ones. People send nice Valentine cards to each other, too.

- cook special food
- play fun games
- wear special clothes
- give gifts
- spend time with family and friends
- clean and decorate the house
- make wishes
- have a party
- help the poor

03 What's the weather like?

Lesson Focus

- **01** Discussing weather conditions, temperature, and seasonal climates
- **02** Talking about people's favorite weather and seasons
- **03** Discussing activities based on weather conditions and seasons
- **04** Using weather related adjectives

UNIT 03 What's the weather like?

Get started

A. Countries around the world have different weather conditions in the same month. See how the weather in July is different in the following three cities. Then answer the questions below with your classmates.

Weather in July

In Toronto, July is hot and humid. The average temperatures are 21°C to 27°C. It sometimes rains.

Beijing's weather in July is hot and humid. The average temperatures in July range from 25°C to 26°C.

For Sydney, July is the coldest month. It is mildly cool with average temperatures ranging from of 8°C to 16°C.

ⓐ How's the weather in your city in July?
ⓑ Which city's weather is similar to the weather in your city?

B. The weather is different in each season. Choose the proper words from the list to describe the weather conditions in each season.

spring

summer

autumn / fall

winter

- sunny   • cloudy   • clear   • windy   • rainy   • snowy   • hot
- warm   • cool   • cold   • freezing • dry   • humid   • muggy

Talk together 🎧

Listen to the dialogue and practice.

John: Hi, Vanessa. How's everything?
Vanessa: It's going well. How are you doing?
John: I'm okay. The university vacation just started. How's the weather in London?
Vanessa: Today? Bad. It's 5 degrees and raining heavily.
John: No kidding. It's sunny and mild here in Madrid. It must be hard for you because you don't like feeling cold.
Vanessa: That's right. How about you?
John: I don't mind cold weather. So what kind of weather do you like?
Vanessa: I like sunny and warm weather. That's why spring is my favorite season.
John: Me, too. What do you like to do in the spring?
Vanessa: Many things. But most of all, I like to go cycling along the river.

Language focus

How's the weather? What's the weather like?	It's raining / snowing. It's warm, cloudy and windy.
What's the temperature?	It's 30 degrees Celsius/Fahrenheit. It's seven degrees below zero Celsius.
What kind of weather do you like? What do you like to do on a sunny day?	I like sunny days. (I like sunny weather.) I like to go on a picnic on a sunny day.
What's your favorite season? What season do you like best?	My favorite season is spring. I like summer best.
What do you like to do in the spring?	I like to go on a picnic.

Practice more

A. Listen to people talking about the weather. Match the pictures with the proper descriptions.

B. Look at the pictures in Part **A** again. With a partner, talk about the weather in pictures.

> **A:** How's the weather? (What's the weather like?)
> **B:** It's raining.
> **A:** What's the temperature?
> **B:** It's 25°C. (It's 77°F.)

C. With your partner, talk about the kind of weather you like. Use the expressions in the box if needed.

> **A:** What kind of weather do you like?
> **B:** I like rainy days.
> **A:** What do you like to do on a rainy day?
> **B:** I like to listen to music.

• go bike riding	• get a suntan	• go hiking	• watch movies
• hang out with friends	• stay home	• read	• listen to music

26 • UNIT 03

Let's do it 1 🎧

A. Listen to today's weather forecasts for a number of cities around the world. Fill out the chart below with the information you hear.

Cities	Today's Conditions	Today's Temperature
San Francisco	_____ and warm	High: 57°F
Paris	Rainy and _____	High:
Auckland	Partly _____	High:
Hong Kong	Hot and _____	High:
Toronto	_____	High:

B. Work in pairs. Talk about what the weather is like in each city and the kind of weather you like. Follow the example.

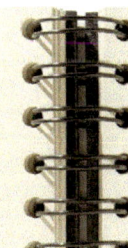

A: What's the weather like in Paris today?
B: It's raining.
A: And what's the temperature?
B: It's 13°C.

A: Which city's weather do you like best?
B: I like the weather in San Francisco best.
A: Why do you like it?
B: Because I like warm weather.

C. Find out today's weather forecasts for three other cities around the world. Make a chart like the one in Part **A** and talk about the weather in each city. Follow the example in Part **B**.

Cities	Today's Conditions	Today's Temperature

Let's do it 2

A. Listen to four people talking about their favorite seasons. Fill in the table below based on what you hear.

		Olivia	Matt	Angela	Joel
1	City			Glasgow	
2	Favorite season				
3	Weather conditions				

B. Listen again and check(✓) the things that they don't like to do in their favorite seasons.

Olivia
- go swimming
- go scuba diving
- relax at home
- go camping

Matt
- go hiking
- go camping
- go fishing
- go for a drive

Angela
- go hiking
- go skiing
- go for a drive
- go cycling

Joel
- go hiking
- go for a walk
- go to a baseball game
- go camping

C. Work with a partner. Talk about the favorite seasons of the people above and the things they like to do in those seasons. Follow the example.

> **Example**
>
> A: Where does Sarah live?
> B: She lives in Seoul.
> A: What's her favorite season?
> B: It's summer.
> A: How's the weather in the summer there?
> B: It's very hot and muggy.
> A: What does she like to do in the summer?
> B: She likes to go swimming and camping.

Reading

A. The following articles say what the weather is like in Costa Rica and the Arctic. Compare the climates of the two regions.

Weather in Costa Rica

Costa Rica is a tropical paradise of Central America. It has a winterless climate with only two seasons; wet or dry. The dry season is from mid-Novemver to May. During the wet season, the majority of rain falls late in the afternoons. Temperatures range between 60°C and 79°F.

Weather in the Arctic

The coldest temperature in the Arctic is -68°C. The Arctic is usually colder but less windy than Antarctica. Also, blizzards are less common in the Arctic. Living in the Arctic would be difficult because of the cold and fog. However, it would be better than living in Antarctica.

B. Answer the following questions with your partner.

1. What are common tropical weather conditions?
2. What's the difference between the weather in Costa Rica and the Arctic?
3. Which do you like better, tropical weather or cold weather?
4. Which place do you think is better for people to live in, tropical countries or cold countries?

Writing

A. Discuss these questions with your partner.

1. What kind of weather do you like?
2. What do you like to do in your favorite kind of weather?
3. Which season do you like best?
4. What do you like to do during that season?

B. Write about the kind of weather you like and your favorite season based on the answers to the questions above.

Example

I like hot and sunny weather, so my favorite season is summer. On really hot days, I like going swimming or drinking lemonade under the shade of a tree in a park. In summer, I always go on camping trips in the mountains or to the beach. When it's not too hot, I also like to go outside and play sports like basketball. Sometimes I have a barbecue with friends.

04 What does it look like?

Lesson Focus

01 Describing shapes, colors and materials
02 Describing uses of objects
03 Making comparisons
04 Asking for and talking about preferences
05 Using *wh*-questions in the simple present tense

UNIT 04 What does it look like?

Get started

A. Can you see the differences between these two objects? They are different in shape, color, material, and use. Choose the correct words from the box below to describe each object and complete the sentences.

It's _____ and _____.
It's made of _____.
It's used for _____.

It's _____ and _____.
It's made of _____.
It's used for _____.

- rectangular
- making phone calls
- pink
- paper
- plastic
- green
- packing gifts
- round

B. Compare the differences among these computers. Complete the sentences below.

- Which computer is bigger, the PC or the laptop?
  The PC is bigger than the laptop.

- Which one is more powerful, the PC or the laptop?
  _____ is _____ than _____.

- Which one is newer, the PC or the PDA?
  _____ is _____ than _____.

- Which one is the handiest?
  _____ is _____.

Talk together

Listen to the dialogue and practice.

Jason: I can't find the USB flash drive I got yesterday.
Molly: Oh, where did you put it?
Jason: I put it in the top drawer.
Molly: Did you check the other drawers? Let me help you find it.
Jason: Thanks.
Molly: Sure. What does it look like? There is a lot of stuff in here.
Jason: It's red, made of rubber, and looks like a beetle.
Molly: It looks like a beetle?
Jason: Yeah, there are many kinds of USBs in various shapes and sizes.
Molly: Is that so? That's interesting. Oh, here it is. Is this yours?
Jason: Oh, that's not mine. Mine is bigger than that one.
Molly: There's another one here. Is this what you're looking for?
Jason: Right, that's it. Thanks a lot.

Language focus

Describing things

What does it look like?
  It's round / square / rectangular / triangular / oval / box-shaped / flat.

What is it made of?
  It's made of wood / plastic / metal / leather / glass.

What do you use it for?
  We use it for making (to make) food.

What is it used for? (What is it for?)
  It's used for (It's for) making food.

Comparing things

Which car is bigger, a sports car or a van?
  A van is bigger than a sports car.

Is the sports car as big as the van?
  No, it's smaller than the van.

Which car is the most expensive?
  The van is the most expensive.

Practice more

A-1. Do you know what each object is called? Choose the correct name of each one from the list and write it in the blank. And what is each object used for? Match each one with the correct use.

Names of items	• vacuum cleaner • digital camera	• MP3 player • blender	• microwave oven • soccer ball	• cooking pot • washing machine
Uses	❶ listen to music ❺ play soccer	❷ vacuum the house ❻ take pictures	❸ heat up food ❼ cook food	❹ wash clothes ❽ mix food together

A-2. With a partner, talk about what each object looks like and what it is used for.

Example

A: What does it look like?
B: It's white, and box-shaped.
A: What is it used for? (What do you use it for?)
B: It's used for heating up food. (We use it for heating up food.)

B. Compare each pair of the items and answer the following questions. The first one is done for you.

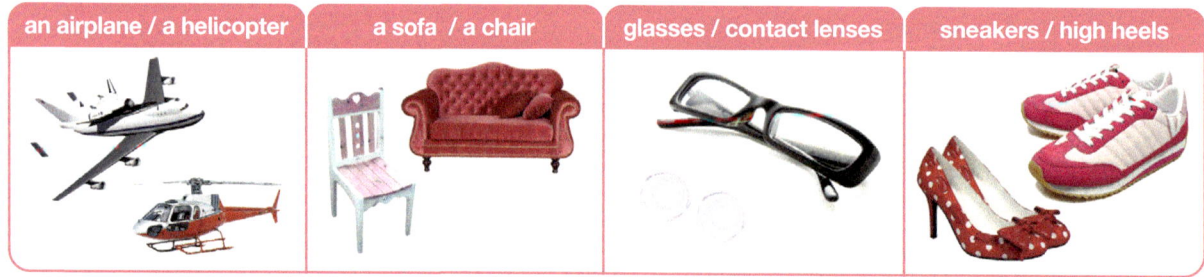

❶ Which one is faster?   An airplane is faster than a helicopter.
❷ Which one is heavier?
❸ Which ones are lighter?
❹ Which ones are more comfortable?

Let's do it 1

A. Listen to the descriptions of the items in the picture. Put the number of the description on the correct picture.

alarm clock   umbrella   flashlight   bag   humidifier   mop

B. Listen again for what each item is like and what each item is used for. Complete the sentences in the table.

flashlight	It is _____ and has a _____ bulb in it. It is used for lighting _____ places.
humidifier	It is made of _____. It has _____ in it. It is used for adding moisture to the _____.
alarm clock	It is _____ and has _____ on it. It helps you _____ in the morning.
mop	It is _____ and made of _____ and cloth. It is used for _____ the floor.
laptop bag	It is _____ and _____. It has a _____ strap. It is made of _____. It is used for _____ a laptop computer.
umbrella	It is _____ and _____. It has a _____. It is used to protect you against the _____ or _____.

C. Work with a partner. Take turns choosing one of the items above and guessing what the item is. Follow the example below. Then try more with some other items of your own.

Example

A: What does it look like?
B: It's long and pointy. It has a handle.
A: What do you use it for?
B: I use it to protect me against the rain or snow.
A: Is it an umbrella? (Is it a mop?)
B: That's right. (That's wrong. Try one more time.)

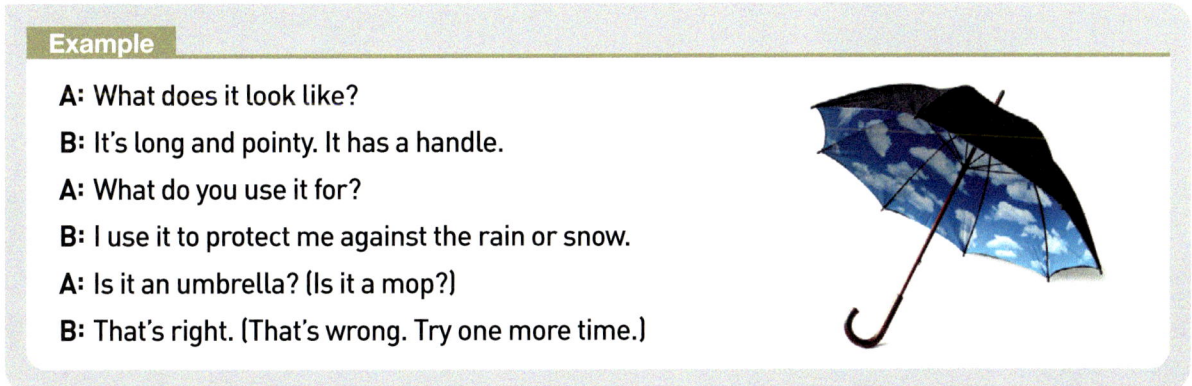

Let's do it 2

A. How are the two items different? Compare the items by completing the sentences using the adjectives below.

① A PDA is _____ than a personal planner.

② A laptop computer is _____ than a desktop computer.

③ An SUV is _____ than a mid-sized sedan.

- convenient
- handy
- practical
- expensive
- durable
- economical

B. People are talking about buying one of the two items above. Listen to the conversations and fill in the table.

Conversation	They are going to buy...	Reasons
1		
2		
3		

C. Work with a partner. Talk about which of the two items in Part **A** you would like to buy and the reasons why you like the item better. Follow the example below.

Example

A: Which one would you like to buy, a PDA or a personal planner?

B: I'd like to get a personal planner.

A: Why do you like it better?

B: It's more economical than a PDA. It's a lot cheaper.
Also, it's more convenient.
I don't have to learn how to use it.
That's why I like a personal planner better.

Reading

A. Have you heard of a Robopet? What do you think it is? Read about Robopet in the following passage.

What would you choose, a Robopet or a real pet?

What could possibly be better than owning a real pet? Owning a Robopet! Robopet is a robotic dog that looks, feels, and acts just like a real dog but is more economical, cleaner, and quieter. First of all, with Robopet, you never have to worry about buying dog food or paying costly vet bills. Secondly, caring for a Robopet is less work because it will never leave a mess. And because Robopet is quieter than a real dog, you don't have to worry about your neighbors complaining about your dog barking all day. Robopet is just as cute, curious, and playful as a real dog. Robopet can bark, roll-over, and even play dead! So, why settle for a pricier, messier, and louder real dog when you can have Robopet at a much lower cost-less than $100! Robopet is just as loyal and lovely as a real dog but is simply more practical and convenient to care for. Plus, your Robopet will live much longer than a real dog. If you are feeling lonely but don't have time to care for a pet, Robopet is perfect for you. Let Robopet be your new best friend!

B. With your partner, answer the following questions.

1. Have you ever seen a Robopet? What do you think of it?
2. What are the good things about keeping a Robopet?
3. What are the bad things about keeping a real dog?
4. How is a Robopet different from a real pet?
5. Which do you like better, a Robopet or a real dog? Why?

Writing

A. Have you ever replaced something old with something new? Answer the questions below, then write a paragraph based on your answers.

1. What did you buy to replace the old item?
2. Why did you want to replace the old one?
3. What does the new item look like?
4. What do you use the new item for?
5. How are the old item and the new item different? Use comparatives in your answers.

Example

I bought a new cell phone recently. I had one, but it was getting old and breaking down a lot. My new cell phone is pink and has many functions. I use it for talking to clients and sending text messages. Because I'm a sales manager, it's important to be in touch with clients. My new cell phone is much lighter than the old one and more convenient to use.

05 Do you have any plans for the weekend?

Lesson Focus

01 Talking about weekend plans and vacations
02 Talking about schedules and future plans
03 Discussing hopes and New Year's resolutions
04 Making future plans with *be + going to* and *be planning to*

UNIT 05 Do you have any plans for the weekend?

Get started

A. Do you have any plans for your next vacation? If you have already made plans, what are you going to do? If you haven't made plans yet, what do you want to do? List them in the chart. You may use the expressions below.

What are you going to do?	What do you want to do?

- ⓐ travel abroad
- ⓑ visit hometown
- ⓒ work around the house
- ⓓ take a class
- ⓔ stay home and relax
- ⓕ spend time with family
- ⓖ make a home page
- ⓗ go on a camping trip / take a short trip
- ⓘ play sports
- ⓙ go hiking in the mountains

B. Around the end of the year or before New Year's Day, many people make resolutions for the new year. Imagine that now you're making New Year's resolutions. Check what you want to do on the list below. If you have your own resolutions, add them.

1. study a foreign language
2. lose / gain weight
3. study abroad
4. get some exercise
5. get married
6. find a boy / girlfriend
7. start a hobby
8. buy a car
9. get a job / change jobs
10. learn to drive

Other resolutions:

Talk together 🎧

Listen to the dialogue and practice.

Alex: Do you have any plans for the winter vacation?
Brenda: I'm going snowboarding with my friends.
Alex: That must be exciting. Where are you going to go?
Brenda: We're going to Lake Valley Resort. Would you like to join us?
Alex: That would be great! But it depends on the date you are leaving and how long you plan to stay there.
Brenda: We are going to leave on January 15th and come back on the 19th.
Alex: Then I can make it. I think I can reschedule my work.
Brenda: Sounds perfect. We plan to stay in a condominium, so each of us needs to bring some food.
Alex: I'd like to get some ready-made pumpkin pies and fruit.
Brenda: That'll be good.

Language focus

Do you have any plans for this weekend? What are you going to do this weekend?	I'm going to play tennis.
Are you doing anything after work? What are you doing after work?	I'm meeting my boyfriend.
What do you plan to do this summer? What are you planning to do this summer?	I plan to travel abroad. I'm planning to travel abroad.
What do you want to do next year? What would you like to do next year? What do you hope to do next year? What is your new year's resolution?	I want to study Chinese. I'd like to learn to drive. I hope to get married. I want to get a new job.
Why do you want to study Chinese?	Because I need to speak Chinese for my work.

Do you have any plans for the weekend?

Practice more

A. With your partner, talk about what Richard, an insurance agent, is planning to do next week by looking at his schedule below.

SUN.	MON.	TUE.	WED.	THU.	FRI.	SAT.
go hiking with friends	go bowling with co-workers after work	meet a client	go on a blind date		go to a high school reunion	

Example

What is he doing on Tuesday?	→	He's meeting a client.
What is he going to do on Tuesday?	→	He's going to meet a client.
What is he planning to do on Tuesday?	→	He's planning to meet a client.

B. With your partner, practice asking and answering questions about your plans for the future. Use the expressions you learned above.

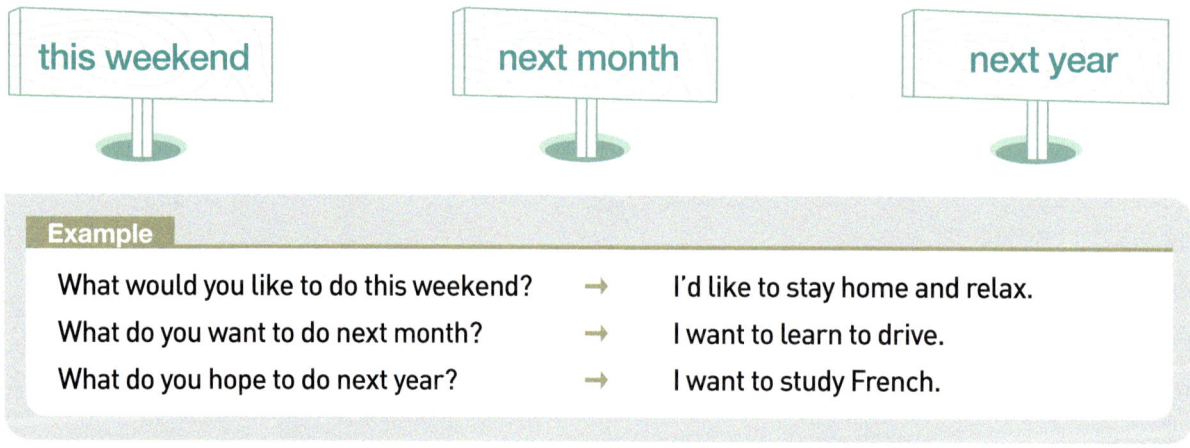

this weekend | next month | next year

Example

What would you like to do this weekend?	→	I'd like to stay home and relax.
What do you want to do next month?	→	I want to learn to drive.
What do you hope to do next year?	→	I want to study French.

C. With your partner, take turns asking and answering questions about your plans at these time periods. Use your own answers.

next week | this summer (winter) | next year

Let's do it 1

A. Imagine that you live in San Francisco and want to attend some events that are going to take place in March. So you'd like to find out information about what kinds of events are going to be held. Listen to part of a radio show that informs people of some of the events not listed on the calendar below. Then write the number of the events on the correct dates.

March San Francisco Events Calendar

SUN.	MON.	TUE.	WED.	THU.	FRI.	SAT.
				1	2	3 Crab Cracking at Seaport Market
4	5	6 Independent Film Festival at Fort Mason Center	7	8	9 Noontime Concert at Old Saint Mary's	10
18	19 Romeo and Juliet at Lincoln Theater	20	21	22	23	24 Antique Craft Fair at Lincoln Park

❶ Magic Show at Berkeley Theatre

❷ Flea Market at Golden Gate Park

❸ Japanese Print Exhibit at the San Francisco Museum of Modern Art

❹ Sunday Brunch Special at the Hilton Hotel

B. Choose some of the events on the calendar you'd like to attend. Then with your partner, talk about your plans to attend those events. Follow the example below.

Example

A: Are there any good events happening in March?

B: Yes, there's one. I'd like to (plan to) go to the antique craft fair.

A: Oh, that sounds fun. When is it going to take place?

B: Saturday, the 24th.

A: Where is it going to be held?

B: It's going to be held at Lincoln Park.

Let's do it 2

A. What do you think your life will be like in the future? What would you like to do in the periods of time listed below? Fill in the chart with your own answers. You may use the expressions given below.

next year	
a couple of years from now	
after graduating	
in ten years	
after you retire	

- run my own business
- buy a house in the country
- change careers
- start a family
- travel around the world
- retire early
- go back to school
- get training for special skills
- get a job
- write my autobiography
- do volunteer work
- learn foreign languages

B. Listen to people talking about their future hopes and plans. Check (✓) if the following statements are **True** or **False**. Then check your answers with your partner.

Conversation		True	False
1	Both of them want to try rock climbing.		
	The woman plans to try scuba diving.		
2	They both would like to have careers.		
	They don't want to get married within five years.		
3	The man hopes to sail his own yacht.		
	The woman would like to paint after she retires.		

C. In pairs, talk about your future plans and hopes using the questions below. When you answer the questions, give details for why you have those plans and hopes.

❶ What do you want to do next year?

❷ What would you like to do three years from now?

❸ What do you hope to do after you retire?

> **Example**
>
> A: What would you like to do three years from now?
>
> B: I'd like to start a family in three years, but my boyfriend and I need to get jobs first. He wants to be a math teacher, and I'd like to work as a web designer. After getting jobs, we're going to start saving money for our wedding and then get married.

Reading

A. Three people (Eric, Jessica, and Tim) are talking about their future dreams. Read their stories and find out what their dreams are like.

My name is Eric. I work at a pizza place to save some money for my classes at a community college. I have to earn quite a bit of money because I'm planning to transfer to a university next year. I'd like to study economics after I get into university. I eventually want to become a financial analyst to help people invest money in growing industries and make them financially secure.

I'm Jessica Grey, and I work as a cook at an Italian restaurant downtown. It's been over four years now since I started working here. I have a dream to open my own restaurant in the next ten years. I'd like to turn the restaurant into a chain with restaurants all over the country. That way, many people can enjoy the food that I make.

I'm Tim, a 26 year-old working as a meteorologist for a TV station. I studied astronomy in college. I've always wanted to be an astronaut. So, I have put my plans into action. Recently, I applied for a competition where NASA selects some people to train at an astronaut training camp. I hope I will be selected for the position. I want to see what the earth looks like from the space. I also want to help with the exploration of other planets.

B. With your partner, answer the following questions.

❶ If you are going to school, what do you want to do after graduation?

❷ If you are thinking of a career change, what would you like to do?

❸ Do you have any special plans for the near future? What do you want to do?

❹ Do you have any long-term dreams? What do you hope to do?

Writing

A. Do you have any dreams for the near or distant future? Choose one of your dreams and write about it.

Example

Right now, I am an office worker at a trading company. I like my job, but someday I'd like to move back to the countryside and settle down there. When I reach my fifties, I'd like to live in a log house in the country and farm for a living. I want to grow seasonal fruit like strawberries and melons. I also hope to have my own orchard and grow apples and peaches there.

06 What kind of dress are you looking for?

Lesson Focus

01 Using shopping related expressions
02 Buying and selling items
03 Talking about different store types and sales
04 Describing problems with purchased items
05 Returning, exchanging and refunding purchased items
06 Making requests

UNIT 06 What kind of dress are you looking for?

Get started

A. Where do you buy the items in the list? Write the items under the correct store type.

- cosmetics
- carpet
- dishwasher
- keyboard
- humidifier
- sweat pants
- shovel
- shampoo
- dumbbells
- binders

| Drugstore | Hardware store | Sporting goods store | Appliances store | Office supplies store |

What else can you buy in each store? Write more items under each category.

B. What's wrong with these items? Choose the correct words that describe the problems with each item.

- tight
- baggy
- broken
- torn
- missing a button
- too long

Talk together

Listen to the dialogue and practice.

Salesperson: Hello. Can I help you with something?
Michael: Yes, I'm looking for a sweater.
Salesperson: We carry a great selection of sweaters. Is there a particular style that you have in mind?
Michael: No, I don't have a style in mind.
Salesperson: Then what size do you wear?
Michael: I wear size 8.
Salesperson: How about this navy one? You can try it on.
Michael: Well, I don't think navy suits me. Does this come in green?
Salesperson: Sure. Here you are.
Michael: Good. I'll take this one.
Salesperson: That's a great choice. And is there anything else I can help you with?
Michael: Actually, there is. Can I get a refund for these pants?
Salesperson: Sure. Do you have the receipt?
Michael: Here you are.

Language focus

Can I help you with something? What can I do for you?	I'm looking for a wool sweater. I'm just looking, thanks.
Do you have (carry) this in size six (red)? Does this come in size six (red)?	Yes, we do. / No, we don't. Yes, it does. / No, it doesn't.
I'd like to exchange this for another one. Can you exchange this for another one?	OK. We can exchange it. I'm sorry. There are no exchanges allowed.
I'd like to return this for a refund. Can I get a refund for this?	OK. We can give you a refund. I'm sorry. We don't give refunds.
What's the problem with it? What's wrong with it?	It's too big for me. The zipper is broken.

Practice more

A. Julia is shopping at a department store with her shopping list. With a partner, take turns being Julia and a salesperson. Make dialogues like the example below.

Things to buy:
1. pink dress (size 6)
2. black leather boots (size 6 1/2)
3. yellow sweater (medium)
4. brown jacket (large)
5. green blouse (size 4)
6. grey suit (size 8)

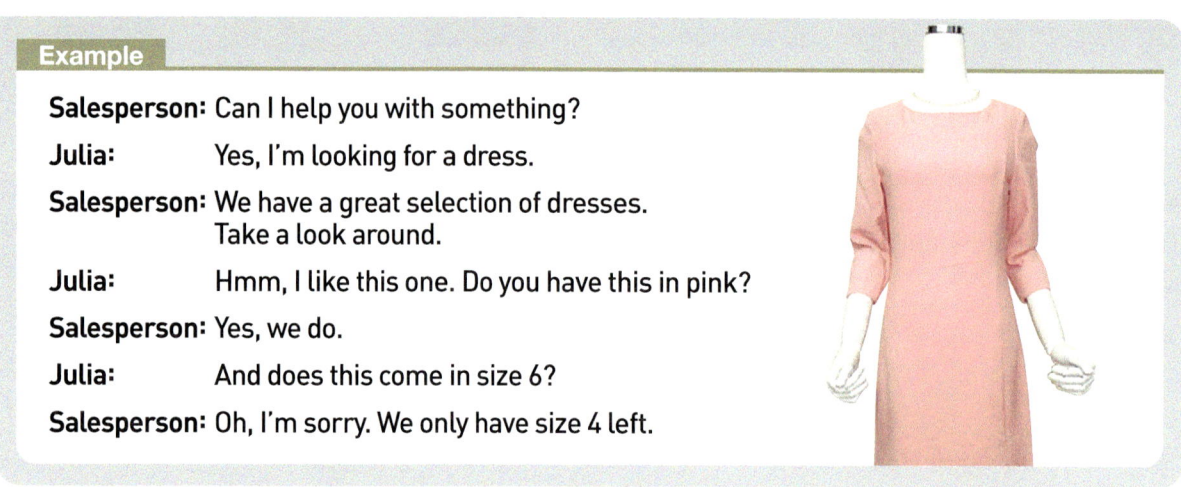

Example

Salesperson: Can I help you with something?
Julia: Yes, I'm looking for a dress.
Salesperson: We have a great selection of dresses. Take a look around.
Julia: Hmm, I like this one. Do you have this in pink?
Salesperson: Yes, we do.
Julia: And does this come in size 6?
Salesperson: Oh, I'm sorry. We only have size 4 left.

B. Julia wants to exchange or get a refund for the things she bought. With a partner, practice the dialogue by replacing the underlined words.

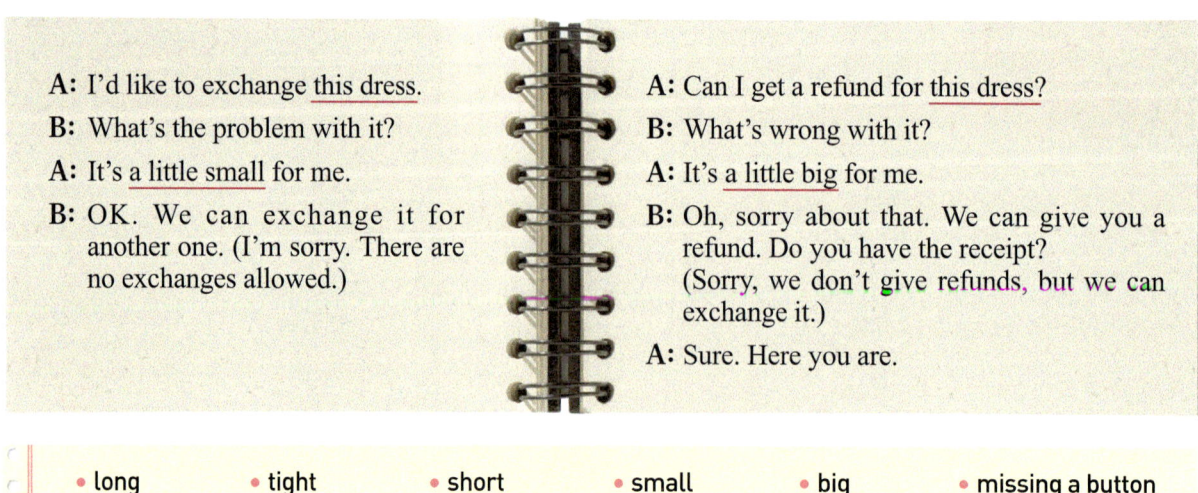

A: I'd like to exchange this dress.
B: What's the problem with it?
A: It's a little small for me.
B: OK. We can exchange it for another one. (I'm sorry. There are no exchanges allowed.)

A: Can I get a refund for this dress?
B: What's wrong with it?
A: It's a little big for me.
B: Oh, sorry about that. We can give you a refund. Do you have the receipt? (Sorry, we don't give refunds, but we can exchange it.)
A: Sure. Here you are.

- long
- tight
- short
- small
- big
- missing a button

Let's do it 1 🎧

A. There's a big year-end sale going on at Oak Valley Shopping Mall. Listen to the conversations and write down what the people are going to buy. Then referring to the pictures below, choose the type of store they would buy each item from.

Conversation	Things to buy	Stores
1	a pair of ( )	
2	goose down ( )	
3	a digital ( )	
4	a carry-on ( )	

Luggage store

Home furnishing store

Appliances store

Sporting goods store

B. Listen to the conversations again and fill in the chart.

Conversation	Size / Color / Features	Price paid
1		
2		
3		
4		

C. With your partner, make up dialogues using the information above. Follow the example below.

Example

A: Hello, what can I do for you?

B: I'm looking for rollerblades.

A: Is there a particular style (color, size) you're looking for?

B: I'd like a pair with a metal frame.

A: Then what about these?

B: Oh, they look nice. I like the color too. I'll take them. And how much are they?

A: They were originally 130 dollars but are now on sale for 50% off. So that will be 65 dollars.

Let's do it 2

A. What's wrong with these items? Choose the correct words to describe the problems from the list below.

- dead
- wrong size
- broken
- came off

B. Listen to the conversations between sales representatives and customers. Write down the problems with the items the customers bought. Write down the problem with each item and check (✓) how the problems were taken care of.

Conversation	Problems	Results		
		exchange	get a refund	others
1				
2				
3				
4				

C. With a partner, role-play conversations between a sales representative and a customer about purchase problems. Use the information in Part **A** and **B**. Follow the example below.

Example

A: Queen's Home Shopping, what can I do for you?

B: Hi, I'd like to exchange (get a refund) for the purse I bought.

A: May I ask what's wrong with it?

B: The strap is torn.

A: Oh, we're very sorry about that. We will exchange that for another one.
　　　　　　　　(We will give you a refurd for that.)

B: Thanks a lot.

Reading

A. Below are two sales flyers and a warranty. What does each piece of information say?

Enjoy a fantastic sales event !

Princess Accessories is closing, so we're going to have a going-out-of business sale from January 10th through to the 16th. Drop by and enjoy the chance to get 50% to 70% off all items in the store. Great selections of accessory items are available including men's accessories. So hurry up! The store is located between Prince Street and 6th Avenue.

[PC Warranty & Support]

All our standard PCs come with:

1. A FIVE-year warranty that covers labour
   The first twelve months also cover parts.
2. Unlimited free upgrades
   - Pay only for parts; the labour is free of charge!
3. Unlimited free online support via our website

Welcome to Doug's Hobby Shop

It's been 30 years since we opened this retail store. Our goal is to complete customer satisfaction. We carry various kinds of hobby items such as model planes, helicopters, boats, and cars as well as all kinds of parts. Please stop by. It's located near the Washington State Convention Center.

B. Answer the following questions with your partner.

1. What benefits can customers get by visiting Princess Accessories?
2. What is covered in the five-year warranty?
3. What kinds of items does Doug's Hobby Shop carry?
4. Do you often go shopping at stores with sales?
5. Do you check the warranty of items before you buy them?
6. Do you collect anything? If so, do you buy items for this collection?

C. Make your own sales flyer by using the examples above.

Writing

A. Have you ever gotten a refund for or exchanged something you bought? Write about this experience below.

Example

About a month ago, I bought two items on a TV home shopping show. I ordered a red sweater and a white shirt. A week later, I got the wrong items. The sweater was black and the shirt was different from the style that I saw on the show. So, I exchanged the sweater for a red one and got a refund for the shirt.

07 What do you think of jazz?

Lesson Focus

- 01 Expressing likes and dislikes
- 02 Talking about free time activities
- 03 Asking for and giving opinions
- 04 Talking about favorite types of entertainment

UNIT 07 What do you think of jazz?

Get started

A. What kind of music, movies, TV shows, and sports do you like? Check your favorites in each category.

Music	Movies	TV shows	Sports
classical ☐	comedy ☐	talk show ☐	bowling ☐
gospel ☐	drama ☐	sitcom ☐	swimming ☐
jazz ☐	science fiction ☐	game show ☐	tennis ☐
Latin ☐	animation ☐	documentary ☐	basketball ☐
rock ☐	adventure ☐	soap opera ☐	soccer ☐
pop ☐	action ☐	news ☐	skiing ☐
hip-hop ☐	western ☐	cartoon ☐	volleyball ☐
rap ☐	horror ☐	sports program ☐	baseball ☐

B. What do you like to do in your free time? Check the activities you like to do and write them down in the box below. If you do any activities other than those in the list, add them. Then with your partner, talk about the things you like to do in your free time.

- play sports
- chat on-line
- read
- go dancing
- cook
- play computer games
- go shopping
- listen to music
- watch movies
- go for a drive
- watch sports
- talk on the phone
- play musucal instruments
- paint
- take pictures

In my free time, I like to...

Talk together 🎧

Listen to the dialogue and practice.

Judy: So, what do you think of Singapore?
Chris: I really like it. I love the clean streets and nice people.
Judy: I agree. So, what do you do in your free time?
Chris: I usually play sports. Sometimes I go to the movies with friends.
Judy: Really! What kind of sports do you like to play?
Chris: Many kinds. I like to play basketball, soccer, tennis and so on.
Judy: By the way, why don't we go for lunch together?
Chris: Sure, what kind of food do you like?
Judy: I like Chinese. How about you?
Chris: Oh, I'm crazy about Chinese.
Judy: Are you? Let's go to my usual place. The food there is fantastic.

Language focus

Do you like jazz? Do you like going to concerts? Do you like to go to concerts?	Yes, I do. / I like it a lot. / I (really) like it. No, I don't. / I don't like it (at all).
How do you like jazz? What do you think of jazz?	I love it. / I'm crazy about it. It's OK. / It's not bad. I hate it. / I can't stand it. I think it's great / terrible / boring.
What kind of sports do you like? What kind of sports do you like to play?	I like tennis. I like to play tennis.
What is your favorite sport? Who is your favorite tennis player?	My favorite sport is tennis. Andre Agassi is my favorite tennis player.

Practice more

A. With your partner, take turns asking and answering questions about the following activities.

jazz
plays
musicals
soap operas
classical music
horror movies
talk shows

shopping online
studying English
dancing
watching TV
listening to music
going to the movies
playing sports

B. Ask three classmates about how they like the activities listed above. Fill in the chart with the activities they like to do.

	Name	The activities they like to do
1		
2		
3		

C. Talk to three other classmates. With each of them, take turns finding out each other's favorite kind of movies, music, and sports. Follow the example below.

Example

A: What kind of sports do you like?
B: I like basketball.
A: Who's your favorite basketball player?
B: I like Tim Duncan.

Let's do it 1

A. What kind of music, movies, sports, and TV shows do you like? Which do you dislike? Fill in the table. Use the words you learned in the Part **A** of the *Get started* section.

	Music	Movies	Sports	TV shows
I like…				
I dislike…				

B. A reporter at the university monthly newspaper plans to write an article about the students' likes and dislikes related to entertainment. Listen to him interviewing three students. Fill in the chart below with the kinds of entertainment the three students like.

	Music	Movies	Sports
Grace			
Richard			
Tracy			

C. Now, talk to your partner to find out what kind of music, movies, sports, and TV shows he or she likes and dislikes. Then complete the chart with your partner's answers. Follow the example below.

My partner:	Music	Movies	Sports	TV shows
Likes				
Dislikes				

Example

A: Do you like listening to music?

B: Oh, I love it.

A: What kind of music do you like to listen to?

B: I like jazz. How about you? Do you like listening to music?

A: It's OK.

B: What's your favorite kind of music?

A: I like Latin music. Is there any kind of music you don't like?

B: I hate rock music. I never listen to it. How about you? What do you dislike?

A: I don't really like classical music.

B: Why is that?

A: It's boring.

Let's do it 2

A. People are talking about their favorite pastimes while looking at information about events that will be held this weekend. Listen to the conversations and put the number of the conversation in the correct box.

Weekend Tips

Bruno Theater
Shakespeare's Play
<Hamlet>
Fri - Sun   4:30 p.m. & 7:30 p.m.
Tickets: $10.00
         Students $ 5.00

Soccer Tournament
Saturday
Game starts at 7:30 p.m.
Tickets: Adults $6.00
         Children $4.00

Dance Festival
Jazz, pop, salsa, techno
& many more
Fri - Sun
Tickets: Adults $7.00
         Children $3.00
For more info. call 774-2378

**"Little Princess"
Live Concert**
Hudson Park Stadium
2 concerts only
Fri, Sat: 8:00 p.m.
Tickets: $30.00~$50.00

"The Lion King"
Fri & Sat
5:00 p.m. & 8:00 p.m.
Tickets: Adults $35.00
         Children $25.00

B. Work with a partner. Using the information above, talk about what you think of the activities related to those events and make plans to go to the events. Follow the example below and use the listening scripts from Part **A**.

Example

A: What do you like to do in your free time?

B: I like to go to concerts. What about you? How do you like going to concerts?

A: I love it. So, what kinds of concerts do you like?

B: I like pop concerts.

A: Oh, I like them a lot, too. The pop group, Little Princess has a concert this weekend. Would you like to go this Saturday?

B: Sure. Let me check the time and the ticket price. Hmm. I think I can make it.

Reading

A. These people are talking about the kinds of entertainment they enjoy. Read about what they do and how they enjoy the activities.

I'm crazy about musicals. The other day, I went to see "Mama Mia", the most popular musical this year. I had a great time listening to the wonderful songs. I love musicals because it is so much fun listening to live music, watching the vivid dancing, and seeing the various costumes and stage decorations. I always get a good feeling after seeing musicals. It is a refreshing feeling. That's what I go to musicals for.

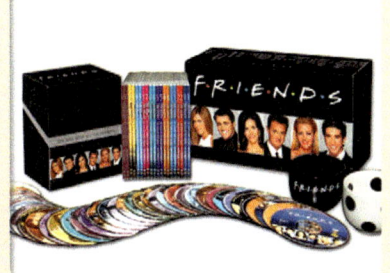

I love collecting romantic comedy DVDs. People think romantic comedy films are just fun. But, there are lots of witty, humorous and dramatic stories in them. Have you seen 'The Wedding Planner', 'Notting Hill' or 'My Best Friend's Wedding'? All of them are romantic comedies! Would you like to start a collection of the best romantic comedies? Just try! Spring is coming and romance is in the air.

I love music. Any kind of music is okay, but what I really like is rock music. I especially like going to concerts. My favorite singer is Robbie Williams. He is the best in the world. I saw his concert live for the first time in Germany a few years ago. I've seen his live concerts three times now. I will go anywhere to see his concert. His music makes me feel excited and happy.

B. With your partner, ask and answer these questions.

❶ What do you think of musicals?
❷ How do you like romantic comedies?
❸ What do you think of rock music?
❹ What kinds of entertainment do you enjoy?
❺ Why do you like to do those activities?

Writing

A. With a partner, take turns asking and answering these questions. Then write down your answers.

① What are the things you like to do in your free time?

② What are the things you would like to do in your free time?
(Those are the things you'd like to do but don't do now.)

B. Write about the things you *like to do* and the things you *would like to do* in your free time.

When I have free time, I usually go for a walk in the park near my place. I walk for about an hour and listen to music on my MP3 player. I like pop and classical music. Also, I like to go to the movies. I like all kinds of movies except horror movies.

In my free time, I'd like to play the piano. I took piano lessons a few years ago, so I know how to play it. I'd like to buy a piano and play it again sometime soon.

08 What would you like to have?

Lesson Focus

01 Talking about food, drinks, recipes and restaurants
02 Reading and ordering from restaurant menus
03 Taking food orders and checking on customers
04 Giving cooking instructions
05 Using the simple present tense

UNIT 08 What would you like to have?

Get started

A. These are famous foods from different countries. Have you tried any of these? Find the correct name of each food from the list. Then talk about the questions below with your classmates.

- Kebab
- burrito
- pho
- sizzling rice soup

Mexico   China   Vietnam   Middle East

❶ Which of the foods have you tried? How do you like it (them)?

❷ Are there any other foods you like from other countries? List them.

❸ What is your favorite traditional food of your country?

B. Choose the proper verb from the list to describe each picture.

- peel
- fry
- add
- bake
- boil
- put in
- stir
- chop
- pour
- slice

Talk together 🎧

Listen to the dialogue and practice.

Waiter: Good evening. Are you ready to order?
Daniel: Yes, I'll have spicy shrimp spaghetti.
Amy: I'd like the chili crab pasta, please.
Waiter: Would you like soup or salad with that?
Daniel: Yes, onion soup, please.
Amy: I'll have Cajun chicken salad.
Waiter: What kind of dressing would you like with that?
Amy: I'd like Ranch.
Waiter: And would you like something to drink?
Daniel: Yes. I'd like a lemon iced tea.
Amy: I'll have an orange juice.
Waiter: OK. So that's spicy shrimp spaghetti, chili crab pasta, onion soup, Cajun chicken salad, one lemon iced tea, and one orange juice.
Daniel: That's right.
Waiter: OK. I'll be right back with your drinks. Thank you.

Language focus

May I take your order? Are you ready to order? What would you like to have?	Yes, I'd like (I'll have) the chili crab pasta. Could we have a few more minutes, please?
Would you like something to drink? What would you like to drink?	Yes, I'd like an orange juice, please. I'll have a lemon juice, please.
Would you like soup or salad?	I'd like crispy chicken salad, please. I'll have mushroom soup, please.
What kind of dressing would you like with that?	I'd like French. I'll have Italian.
Would you care for some dessert?	Yes. I'd like a cheesecake. / No, thank you.
How do you make it?	First, fry onions and peas...

Practice more

A. Imagine that you are at a burger place. With your partner, practice ordering food and drinks from the menu. Use the expressions in the *Language Focus* section.

Menu

Burgers (with fries)
Cheeseburger
Grilled Chicken Burger
Roasted Beef Burger

Salad
Oriental Salad
Green Salad
Mixed Salad
(Dressing: French, Oil and Vinegar, Ranch)

Drinks
Soft Drinks (Coke, Sprite, Root Beer)
Iced Tea
Coffee

Dessert
Cheesecake (Orange, Blueberry)
Soft Ice Cream (Chocolate, Vanilla)

Example

A: May I take your order?
B: I'd like a cheeseburger, please.
A: Would you like anything to drink?
B: Yes, please. I'd like a coke.
A: Would you like salad or dessert with that?
B: No, thank you. I'll just have the burger and drink.
A: All right, sir. That's $6.50.

B. These pictures are describing the procedures for making a banana strawberry yogurt smoothie. Complete the sentences by filling in the blanks with the proper words from the list.

_____ the banana   _____ it   _____ the banana and strawberries in the blender. And _____ the yogurt.   _____ the mixture in the blender.

- blend   - slice   - peel   - put   - add

66 • UNIT 08

Let's do it 1

A. Lisa and Brandon are ordering their lunch at a restaurant. Listen to the conversation and check (✓) the food they ordered from the menu. Then write down the food in the table below.

Lunch Special

Appetizer
Clam Chowder and Garlic Bread
Nachos with Cheese
Fried Calamari

Soup
Mushroom Soup
Creamy Tomato Soup
Potato & Onion Soup

Salad & Dressing
Garden Salad
Crispy Chicken Breast Salad
Tomato and Mushroom Salad
(Dressing: French, Italian, Thousand Island)

Main Course
Sirloin Steak
Grilled Chicken Wings
Smoked Salmon
Pork Tenderloin

Beverages
Iced Tea (lemon, peach)
Ade (orange, mango, citron)
Juice (orange, pineapple)

Desserts
Chocolate Cake
Cheesecake
Ice Cream

	Lisa	Brandon
Food and drinks they ordered		

B. Imagine that you are ordering food at the same restaurant as above. With your partner, make dialogues by taking and giving food orders.

Example

A: Excuse me.
B: Good afternoon. May I take your order?
A: I'd like to start with nachos with cheese.
B: And what would you like for your main course?
A: I'll have smoked salmon.
B: Would you like soup or salad with that?
A: I'll have tomato and mushroom salad.
B: What kind of dressing would you like?
A: Italian, please.
B: Would you like something to drink?
A: I'd like a mangoade, please.
B: Would you care for any dessert?
A: No, thank you.

What would you like to have?

Let's do it 2

A. Listen to the recipe of a dish and complete the ingredients list. Then complete the procedures by filling in the blanks based on what you hear.

Ingredients
- onions
- peas
- soy sauce

Egg Fried Rice with Shrimp

1. _____ onions, carrots, and peas together for _____ minutes.
2. _____ the shrimp with the other _____ and _____ it for another two minutes.
3. _____ two eggs and _____ them into the mixture.
4. _____ it for three minutes then _____ the cooked rice.
5. _____ in a little soy sauce and _____.

B. These pictures show how to make an omelet, but they are not in order. Listen to the recipe and number the pictures in the correct order from 1 to 6.

Making an Omelet

C. With your partner, talk about how to make an omelet by looking at the pictures and using the words given. Refer to the recipe of the food in Part **A**.

- beat
- fold
- break
- heat up
- turn
- pour

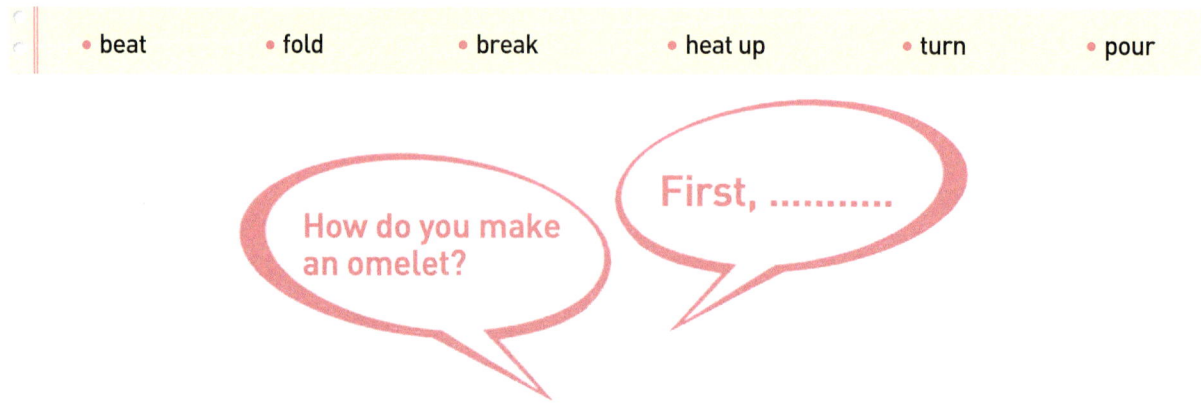

How do you make an omelet?

First, …………

68 • UNIT 08

Reading

A. Do you usually cook or eat out for dinner on the weekend? If you like cooking better, what do you usually cook? If you like eating out better, what do you usually have? Read the passages below.

Have you tried *Okonomiyaki*? *Okonomiyaki* is a Japanese style pancake. *Okonomi* means "what you like" and yaki means "cooked." So *Okonomiyaki* means "cook what you like, the way you like." You can add your favorite ingredients to *Okonomiyaki*. It usually includes chopped cabbage and various toppings like sliced pork, red ginger, corn, green onions, squid, shrimp, bean sprouts, etc. Making *Okonomiyaki* is not difficult. First, mix the flour and eggs well and put a Chinese yam into the mixture. Next, put a small amount of soy sauce and mayonnaise in the mixture. Then cut the cabbage and green onions into small pieces and add them to the mixture. You can add any other vegetables you like. Finally, spread some cooking oil on a heated pan, put the mixture in the pan, and fry it well.

##

Designed in a spacious antique-style, the new Sam's serves Thai dishes. For appetizers, we ordered fried chicken breast with a sweet and sour sauce. They tasted great. The entrees were served in the traditional Thai family style.

A highlight of the menu is the roasted beef wrapped in bacon and served with mashed potatoes and vegetables in a cream sauce. The dish was fantastic.

Sam's Cafe is well known for its desserts, so I'd like to recommend the mocha chiffon. This restaurant made a good start, and time will tell if its success continues.

B. Answer these questions with your partner.

① Which do you like better, eating out or cooking? Why?

② Many people often like eating out lately.
What do you think of eating out? Is it good or bad?

③ What kind of food do you like to eat out?

④ What food do you enjoy cooking?

Writing

A. Answer these questions with your partner.

1 What is your favorite dish? Briefly explain how to make it.

2 What is a healthy food that you like to eat? What is the food good for?

3 Do you like eating out? What's your favorite restaurant? Why do you like to go there?

4 What do you usually order there? Why do you like eating the food?

B. Choose one of the questions above and write about it.

09 Are you under the weather?

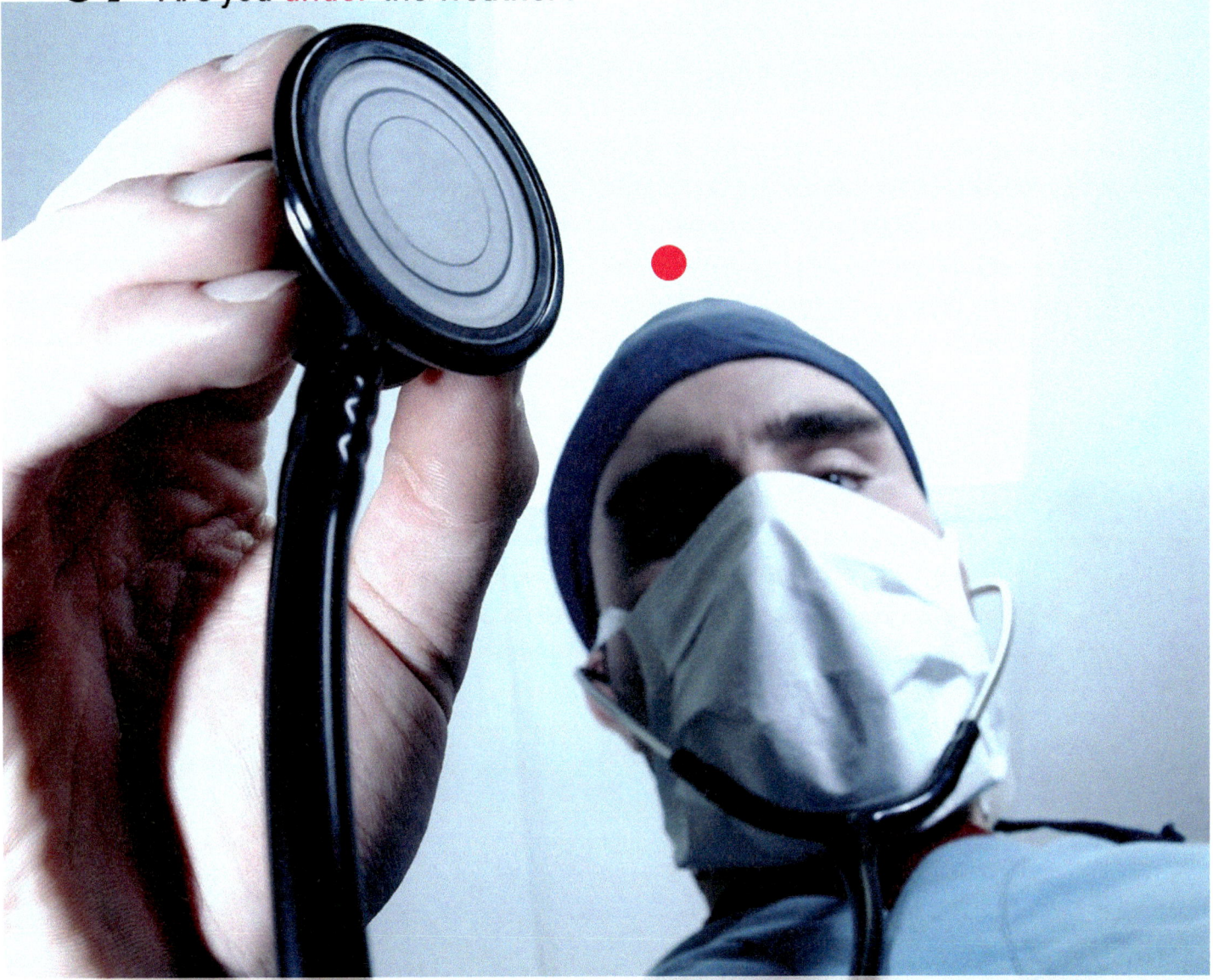

Lesson Focus

01 Talking about illnesses and health problems
02 Describing symptoms
03 Naming specialists
04 Making appointments with medical professionals
05 Giving and receiving advice related to health problems
06 Using affirmative and negative imperatives

Are you under the weather?

Get started

A. What's wrong with these people? Choose the correct medical problem from the list below and write it under the correct picture.

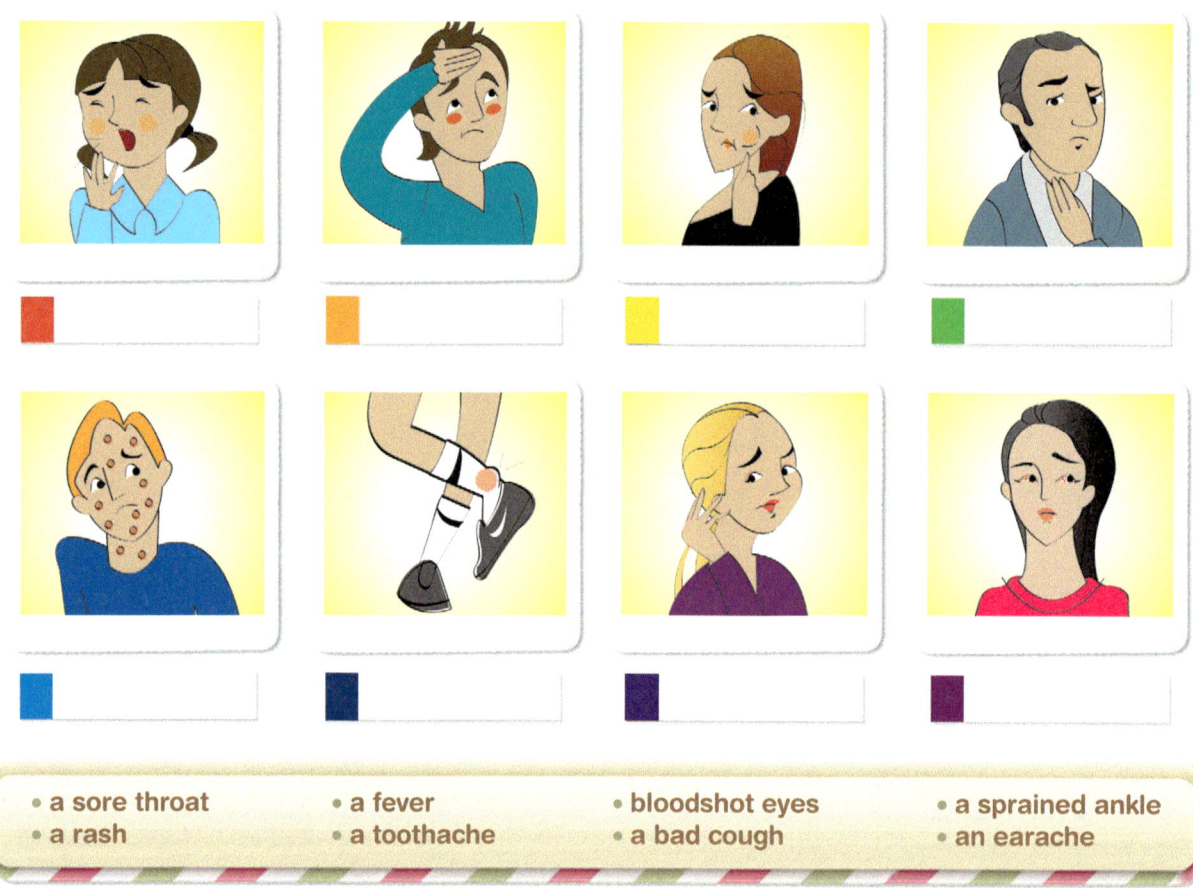

- a sore throat
- a rash
- a fever
- a toothache
- bloodshot eyes
- a bad cough
- a sprained ankle
- an earache

B. It you have the above medical problems, which doctor should you see? Write the problems under the right medical doctor.

Orthopedist	Physician	Dentist	Dermatologist	eye doctor	E.N.T Doctor

Talk together 🎧

Listen to the dialogue and practice.

Dr. Graham: How are you doing, Mandy?
Mandy: I don't feel well.
Dr. Graham: What's the matter?
Mandy: I think I have a cold. I have a sore throat and a runny nose.
Dr. Graham: What else is wrong?
Mandy: I've got a headache and a diarrhea, too.
Dr. Graham: When did this start?
Mandy: Last night.
Dr. Graham: I see. I think you have the flu. I'm going to write you a prescription.
Mandy: Okay. Thank you.
Dr. Graham: You should drink lots of warm water and get plenty of rest. I suggest you take the rest of the day off.
Mandy: That's a good idea. I'll take your advice.

Language focus

What's wrong? What's the matter (problem)? What seems to be the problem?	I have a backache. My back aches. My head hurts.
What else is wrong?	I have a fever, too.
When did it (this) start?	Last night. / Two days ago.
I am going to write (give) you a prescription.	Okay. Thank you.
You should drink lots of warm water. You should stay in bed.	I'll take your advice.
Why don't you take the rest of the day off? I suggest you stay at home and relax.	That's a good idea.

Are you under the weather?

Practice more

A. With your partner, take turns asking about health problems using the words below. Follow the example.

> You look sick. Do you feel OK?
>
> No, I don't.
>
> What's the matter?
>
> I have a bad backache.

pale	terrible	a stiff neck	food poisoning
sick	ill	allergies	an upset stomach
awful		insomnia	

B. Work with a partner. Take turns being a patient and a doctor. The patient explains what the problem is and the doctor gives some advice. Follow the example.

Example

Dr. Lee: What seems to be the problem, Jason?

Jason: I have a fever.

Dr. Lee: Let me check. Hmm, it's not bad. You should get some rest and take one aspirin after every meal.

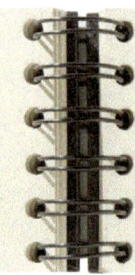

I have a bad cough.	don't lift anything heavy
My whole body aches.	do some neck exercises
I have a backache.	place a hot pack on it
I have a stiff neck.	take some cough syrup
My arm hurts.	stay at home and get enough rest

Let's do it 1

A-1. Match each symptom with the appropriate advice a doctor may give the patient.

- ⓐ a burn
- ⓑ a sore throat
- ⓒ a twisted ankle
- ⓓ the flu

- ❶ get some rest
- ❷ put it in a cast
- ❸ put some ointment on it
- ❹ gargle with salt water

A-2. Listen to the conversations. Put the number of the conversation on the correct picture.

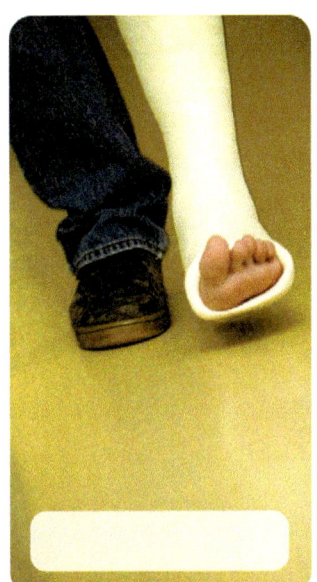 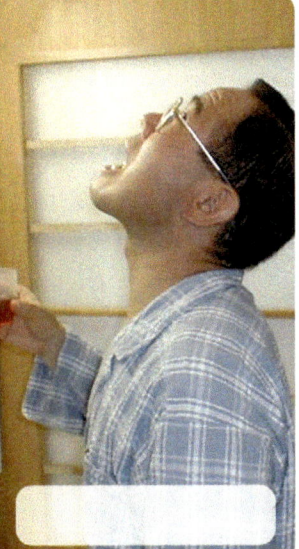  

B. Work with a partner. Make up dialogues like the one in the example using the words given below.

Example

A: Hi, you don't look well. What's wrong?
B: I have a sore throat.
A: I'm sorry to hear that.
B: I don't have time to see a doctor. Could you recommend a good home remedy?
A: Why don't you gargle with salt water?
And you should drink lots of warm water.
B: Thanks, those are good ideas.

insomnia	drink warm water before going to bed.
a bad cold	drink ginger tea and get plenty of rest.
a sunburn	put potato slices on the affected area.
the chills	eat chicken soup.

Are you under the weather? • 75

Let's do it 2

A. When you have these symptoms, which doctor should you see? Match the symptoms with the right doctors.

- ⓐ toothache
- ⓑ pimples
- ⓒ diarrhea
- ⓓ sprained wrist

- ❶ physician
- ❷ dermatologist
- ❸ orthopedist
- ❹ dentist

B. Listen to the conversations between a receptionist and a patient. What's wrong with each patient? Which doctor should they see? Write the number of the conversation on the correct picture.

C. Imagine you are calling to make an appointment to see a doctor. Work with a partner and take turns being the receptionist and the caller. Make dialogues using the listening script from Part **B**. Follow the example below.

> **Example**
>
> **Receptionist:** Hello, what can I do for you?
> **Patient:** I twisted my ankle. I'd like to make an appointment with the doctor.
> **Receptionist:** I'm sorry, but he's all booked today.
> **Patient:** How about tomorrow morning?
> **Receptionist:** Oh, hold on please. You're lucky. Can you come in this afternoon at 3:00?
> **Patient:** That's great. Thank you very much. See you then.

Reading

A. The passages below are from the Q&A section of a health magazine. What are the people's questions? What advice do the answers give?

Dear Dr. Will

Q I have a regular 9 to 6 office job, and it's not bad. For the past few months, however, I've started feeling sleepy, and I get bad headaches, too. I used to eat well, but these days I have lost my appetite. What should I do?

- Tired in San Francisco

A Dear Tired,
Many people are stressed out, and they feel the same way you do. I think stress is a major cause of your symptoms. Try to find good ways to reduce your stress. Taking a short break in the office can help. As a part of your daily routine, try exercising and spending time with friends. This will reduce your stress as well. Listening to classical music is also relaxing. Moreover, try to get a good night's sleep.

Q I got treatment for back pain and tried various therapies. These seemed to help but did not totally clear up the problem. Can you suggest anything else?

- Matthew -

A Dear Matthew,
There are many other traditional therapies for back pain. One of them is acupuncture, where needles are put in people's skin. The needles help the body focus on and relieve the back pain. Aside from back pain, acupuncture can help with various other conditions.

B. Answer these questions with your partner.

1. Do you get stressed out often? What usually makes you stressed out?
2. What do you do to reduce stress?
3. Have you received acupuncture treatment before? If so, was it helpful?
4. What do you think about acupuncture? Would you recommend it to others?

Writing

A. Pretend you are worrying about your weight and would like to use the Internet to ask a doctor for advice. Imagine that you will log on to a website and ask the on-line doctor for advice by writing a letter and posting it on the Q&A section. Ask the doctor for advice about your weight problem. You may use the words in the box below to help you with your letter.

- thin
- slim
- slender
- skinny
- chubby
- fat
- keep in shape
- go on a diet
- get some exercise
- work out
- eat too much
- eat healthy food
- lose weight
- gain weight
- stay healthy

Example

Dear Dr. Phil,

I'm a 23-year-old girl. I have a question about my weight.
I don't eat too much, but, I often feel tired, and I have gained weight.
What is my problem? Should I eat less? Do you think I should see a doctor?
I'm looking forward to hearing from you as soon as possible.
Rachel, Sydney

Dear Dr. Phil,

10 What is your place like?

Lesson Focus

01 Talking about different types of housing
02 Inquiring about renting a home with a real estate agent
03 Reporting problems related to living situations
04 Describing dream homes
05 Using prepositions of place

UNIT 10 What is your place like?

Get started

A. Label the house below with the numbers of the words in the list.

- ❶ garage
- ❷ driveway
- ❸ garden
- ❹ front yard
- ❺ porch
- ❻ backyard
- ❼ balcony
- ❽ patio

B. This picture shows what a typical apartment is like in western countries. Label the apartment with the numbers of the correct words.

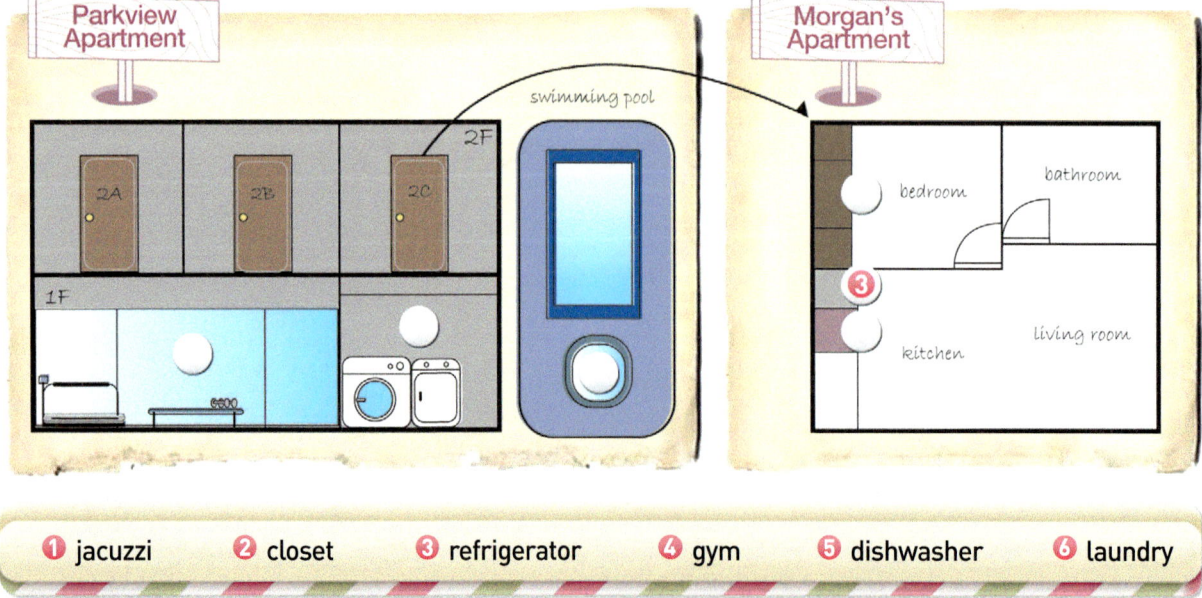

- ❶ jacuzzi
- ❷ closet
- ❸ refrigerator
- ❹ gym
- ❺ dishwasher
- ❻ laundry

Talk together

Listen to the dialogue and practice.

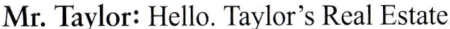

Mr. Taylor: Hello. Taylor's Real Estate. What can I do for you?
Ashley: I'm looking for an apartment in the Concord area.
Mr. Taylor: All right. What kind of apartment do you need?
Ashley: I'd like a two-bedroom apartment.
Mr. Taylor: There's a nice one available.
Ashley: Great. What's it like?
Mr. Taylor: Well, there are two bedrooms; one with a balcony, a large kitchen, a dining room, one bathroom, and a living room.
Ashley: Is it furnished?
Mr. Taylor: Yes, it's fully furnished. Also, there's a big shopping mall close-by.
Ashley: How much is the rent?
Mr. Taylor: 800 dollars a month. Would you like to see it?
Ashley: Yes, can I see it this afternoon?

Language focus

Renting a place	
What kind of apartment do you need?	I need a two-bedroom apartment.
What's the apartment / house like? How many bedrooms are there? (How many bedrooms does it have?)	It's a two-bedroom apartment with a den. It's a studio.
Is it furnished? How much is the rent?	Yes, it's furnished. / No, it's unfurnished. It's 800 dollars a month.

Describing a place	
Do you live in an apartment or a house? Where is your place located?	I live in a house. It's in the suburbs.
Does it have a patio? Is there a park (a beach / a shopping center) nearby?	Yes, it does. / No, it doesn't. Yes, there are three parks nearby. No, there aren't any parks nearby.
What do you like about it?	It has a nice ocean view.

Practice more

A. A customer and a real estate agent are talking on the phone. With a partner, practice the dialogue using the information below.

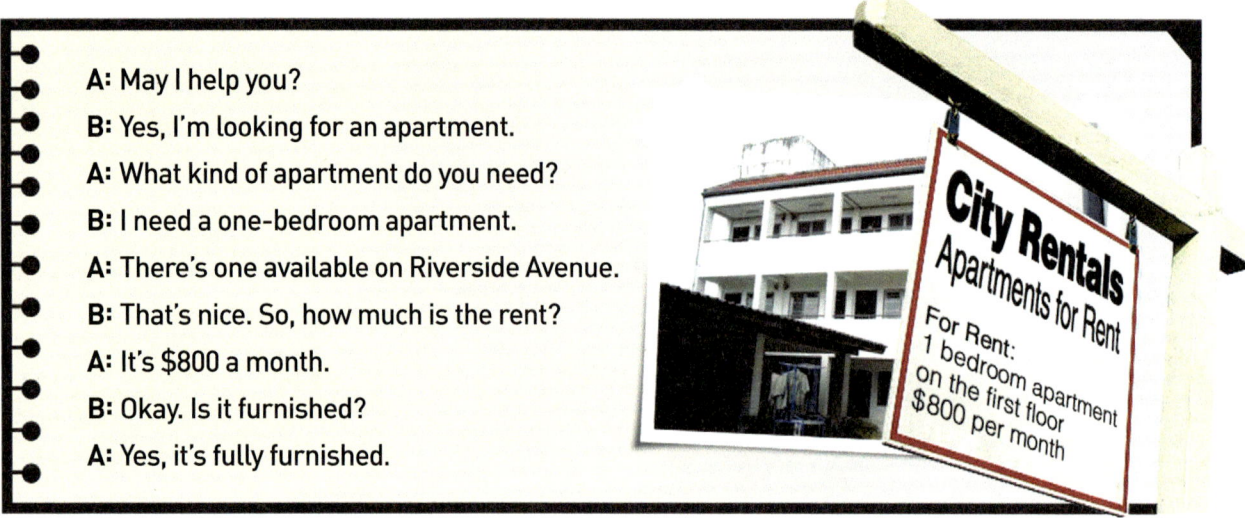

A: May I help you?
B: Yes, I'm looking for an apartment.
A: What kind of apartment do you need?
B: I need a one-bedroom apartment.
A: There's one available on Riverside Avenue.
B: That's nice. So, how much is the rent?
A: It's $800 a month.
B: Okay. Is it furnished?
A: Yes, it's fully furnished.

❶
- two-bedroom house with large kitchen
- on Bank Street
- for $950 a month
- unfurnished

❷
- three-bedroom apartment with two bathrooms
- on Oak Avenue
- for $1,400 a month
- partially furnished

❸
- one-bedroom apartment with a large closet
- on Park Street
- for $600 a month
- fully furnished

B-. Talk to your partner about his/her house or apartment. Complete the table with your partner's answers.

	Questions	Answers
1	Do you live in a house or an apartment?	
2	Where is it located?	
3	How many rooms are there?	
4	What's your favorite room?	

B-. With a partner, take turns asking and answering the questions above using the information about the places below.

Apartment
- on Pine Street
- 1 bedroom, kitchen, 1 bathroom, dining room, living room

House
- on Baker Street
- 2 bedrooms, kitchen, 1 bathroom, living room and dining room

Apartment
- on 12th Avenue
- 2 bedrooms, living room, 2 bathrooms, kitchen,

Let's do it 1

A. Listen to people talking about their places. Fill in the table based on the conversations.

	Conversation 1	Conversation 2	Conversation 3
Location			
Things they like about their places			

B. Work with a partner. Pretend you just moved into a new place and now you are talking to your partner about your new place. Use the example and the information below to help you with your responses.

At the riverside

- three bedrooms, two bathrooms, a big kitchen, a family room, a dining room
- five-minute walk to the shopping mall
- a nice river view, a big patio

In the suburbs

- one bedroom, one bathroom, a small kitchen, a living room
- many parking spaces and a playground
- close to the subway station

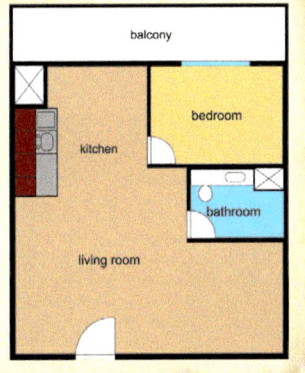

Central downtown area

- a modern bathroom
- a big walk-in closet and a washing machine
- close to Civic Park and Central Library

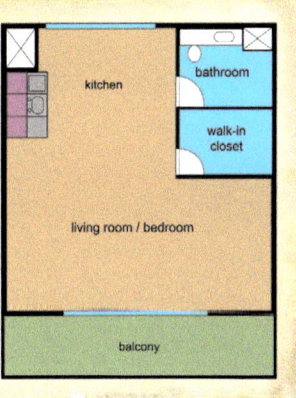

Example

A: Hi, Dora. How do you like your new apartment?

B: I like it a lot!

A: So, what's it like?

B: It has two bedrooms, two bathrooms, a kitchen, and a living room.

A: Where is it located?

B: It's near the downtown shopping district.

A: Sounds great. And what do you like about it?

B: As you know, it's very close to shopping. It has a nice laundry room and a well-equipped gym.

Let's do it 2 🎧

A-①. Tenants and landlords are talking on the phone about the problems in the tenants' apartments. Listen to the conversations and number the pictures.

A-②. Listen again and fill in the chart with the information you hear.

	Problems	The landlord will send ...
1	.... in the hallway aren't working.	
2	The .... stopped working.	
3	The .... overflowed.	

B. Work with a partner. Follow the example and role-play a telephone conversation between a tenant and a landlord. Use the words below.

> **Example**
>
> **A:** Hello.
> **B:** Hi, this is Diana Welch, your tenant in apartment 5.
> **A:** Oh, hi, Diana. What can I do for you?
> **B:** Well, I'm having a problem with the air conditioner. It's not working.
> **A:** Okay. I'll send someone over to take a look.
> **B:** How soon will that be?
> **A:** It will probably be before 2 p.m.
> **B:** Great. Thank you.

- stove
- faucet in the kitchen sink
- shower
- the closet door

- dishwasher
- lock on the front door
- fire alarm
- the dryer in the laundry room

- broken
- fell off
- locked
- not working

84 • UNIT 10

Reading

A. The following are advertisements for renting a house or an apartment. Find meanings of the shortened forms of some of the words in the ads.

Oak Avenue
2 BR apt w/ 1 bath
Carpeted & Furn.
Central air & heat
Util pd. $900 + 1 mo sec dep.
Tel: 709-3652 anytime

Grand Street
3 BR house w/lrg kitchen
Avail immediately
$1,300+util. 1 mo sec dep.
Tel: 510-514-0002
call after 5 p.m.

Lakewood Area
Furn studio apt.
Shared laun & gym in basement
5 min-walk to subway
Quiet Avail 7/2
$450/mo.
Tel: 502-7200 anytime

B. Answer the questions below with a partner.

❶ What does each of these shortened forms stand for?
  br   lrg   util   pd   mo   furn   laun   avail

❷ What does 'sec dep' mean?

❸ How many bedrooms does the house on Grand Street have?

❹ How much do people have to pay for the first month to rent the apartment on Oak Avenue?

❺ What do you think a *Furn studio apt.* is like?

Writing

A. With your partner, talk about your dream house by asking and answering the questions below.

1 Where do you want to live? Would you like to live in the countryside, downtown, or in the suburbs?

2 Would you like to live in a house or an apartment?

3 What kinds of rooms would you like to have in your place?

4 What else would you like to have in your place?

B. Write about your dream house.

My dream house is in the city. It is a two-story house. There are nine rooms altogether. On the first floor, there's a living room, a dining room, a study, and a kitchen. On the second floor, there are three bedrooms and two bathrooms. Every room has a nice view.

Outside the house, there's a big garage. I park my car there. There's also a nice garden. There are many kinds of flowers and plants. There is also a backyard with a swimming pool. In the backyard, I usually have barbecues with friends and family.

11 Who does he work for?

Lesson Focus

01 Talking about occupations and where people work
02 Giving opinions about work
03 Discussing jobs skills and requirements
04 Reading job advertisements
05 Using descriptive adjectives related to occupations
06 Describing one's dream job

UNIT 11 Who does he work for?

Get started

A-1. Choose the proper job titles from the list and write them down under the correct pictures.

Word List
- veterinarian
- security guard
- flight attendant
- interpreter
- receptionist
- librarian

A-2. What does each person do at work? Match each job with the proper description of it.

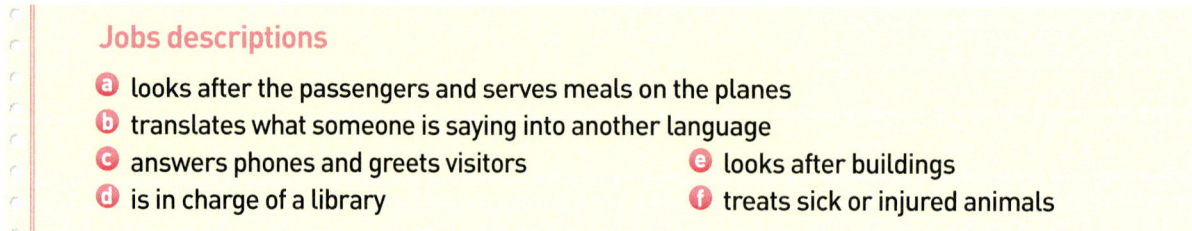

Jobs descriptions
ⓐ looks after the passengers and serves meals on the planes
ⓑ translates what someone is saying into another language
ⓒ answers phones and greets visitors   ⓔ looks after buildings
ⓓ is in charge of a library   ⓕ treats sick or injured animals

B. What do you think of each job below? Which words do you think properly describe each job? Choose the proper words from the list.

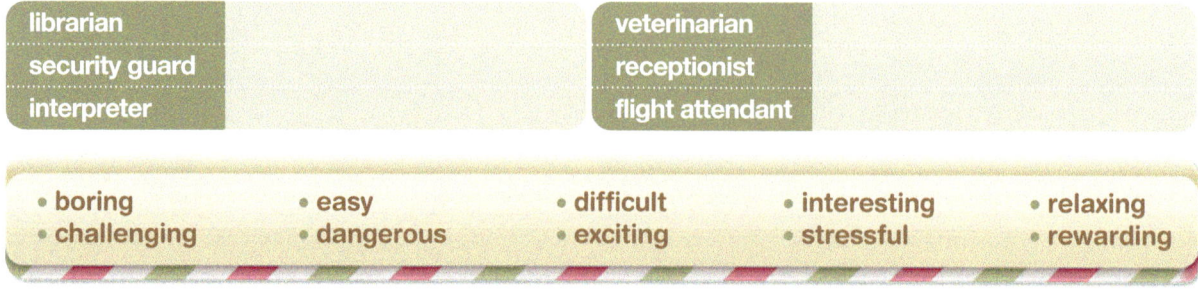

librarian	veterinarian
security guard	receptionist
interpreter	flight attendant

- boring • easy • difficult • interesting • relaxing
- challenging • dangerous • exciting • stressful • rewarding

Talk together 🎧

Listen to the dialogue and practice.

Carly: Hey, Shane, I heard you got a new job. So what do you do, exactly?
Shane: I work as a computer programmer for AT Electronics.
Do you still work as an interpreter?
Carly: Oh, yes! Today, I'm going to attend a conference in Irvine.
Shane: So, how do you like your job?
Carly: Oh, I love my job. How about you?
Shane: It's tough, but I'm doing OK. So, what do you like about your job?
Carly: The trips to many different places, the pay, and meeting many new people.
Shane: Good for you. But it must be difficult balancing both work and family.
Carly: A little bit. My husband helps me a lot, though.
Shane: Well, it's good to hear that you are doing well.

Language focus

What do you do?	I am a computer programmer.
Who do you work for? Where do you work?	I work for (at) AT Electronics.
What are your working hours?	I work Monday through Friday, 9 a.m. to 6 p.m.
How do you like your job? What do you think of your job?	It's exciting and challenging.
Why do you like your job? What do you like about your job?	The good atmosphere, high salary and nice people. There is a good atmosphere, the pay is excellent, and the people are nice.

Practice more

A. With your partner, practice the dialogue using the information given below.

A: What do you do?
B: I'm a waitress.
A: Where do you work?
B: I work at Park Side Cafe.
A: Do you work part-time or full-time there?
B: I am a part-timer. (I work part-time.)
A: What are your (the) working hours?
B: I work from Monday to Friday. I start work at 8 a.m. and finish at 3 p.m.

- security guard
- Ace Entertainment
- part-timer
- Mon. Wed. Fri. 9 p.m.-5 a.m.

- receptionist
- a dental clinic
- full-timer
- Mon. to Fri. 9 a.m.-6 p.m.

- bank teller
- Harris Bank
- part-timer
- Mon. to Fri. 10 a.m.-4 p.m.

B. With your partner, practice the dialogue using the information below.

A: Alex, what do you do?
B: I'm a fashion photographer.
A: What do you think of your job?
B: It's exciting and challenging.
A: What do you like about your job?
B: I meet many famous models and TV stars. I always have to take better pictures of them. I like challenges.

 Ian
Veterinarian
- interesting and rewarding
- like animals and like to take care of them

 Jane
Interpreter
- challenging
- like meeting business people and well-known speakers

 **Tim**
Professor
- exciting and rewarding
- like to teach students and do research in the library

90 • UNIT 11

Let's do it 1

A. Interview your partner with the questions below and write their answers.

	Questions	Answers
1	What do you do?	
2	Who do you work for? (Where do you go to school (college)?)	
3	What exactly do you do at work? (What do you study?)	
4	How do you like your job? (How do you like your major?)	

B. Listen to the conversations and fill out the chart.

	Conversation 1	Conversation 2	Conversation 3	Conversation 4
Jobs				
Work / Major descriptions	learn about _____ and structures	arrange _____ for _____	give customers _____ about their accounts and banking	arrange locations, _____ and decorations
How they like their work/major				

C. Work with a partner. Make up dialogues using the information from Part **B**. Follow the example.

Example

A: What do you do?
B: I'm a party planner.
A: Who do you work for?
B: I am a freelancer.
A: What exactly do you do at work?
B: I make arrangements for party locations, food and decorations.
A: What do you think of your job?
B: It's very fun because I can be creative.

A: What do you do?
B: _____
A: Who do you work for?
   (What school do you go to?)
B: _____
A: What exactly do you do at work?
   (What do you study?)
B: _____
A: How do you like your job?
   (How do you like your major?)
B: _____

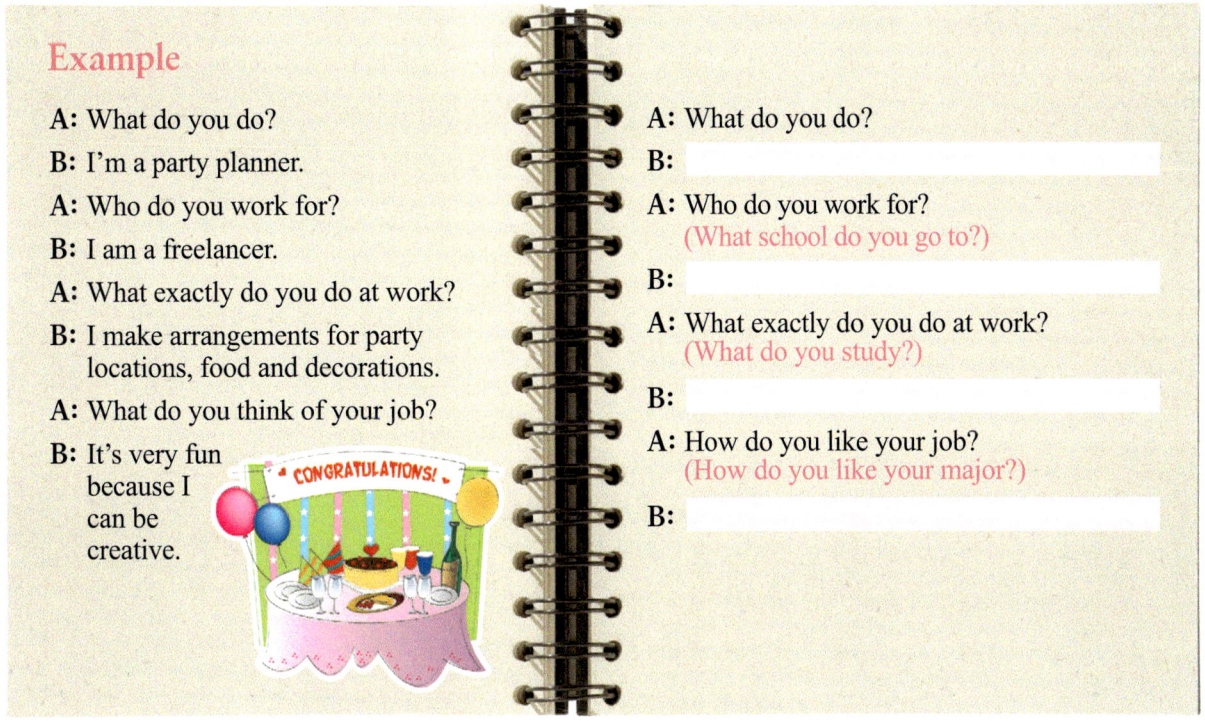

Let's do it 2

A. What qualities should these people have for their jobs? Choose the appropriate words for each person from the list.

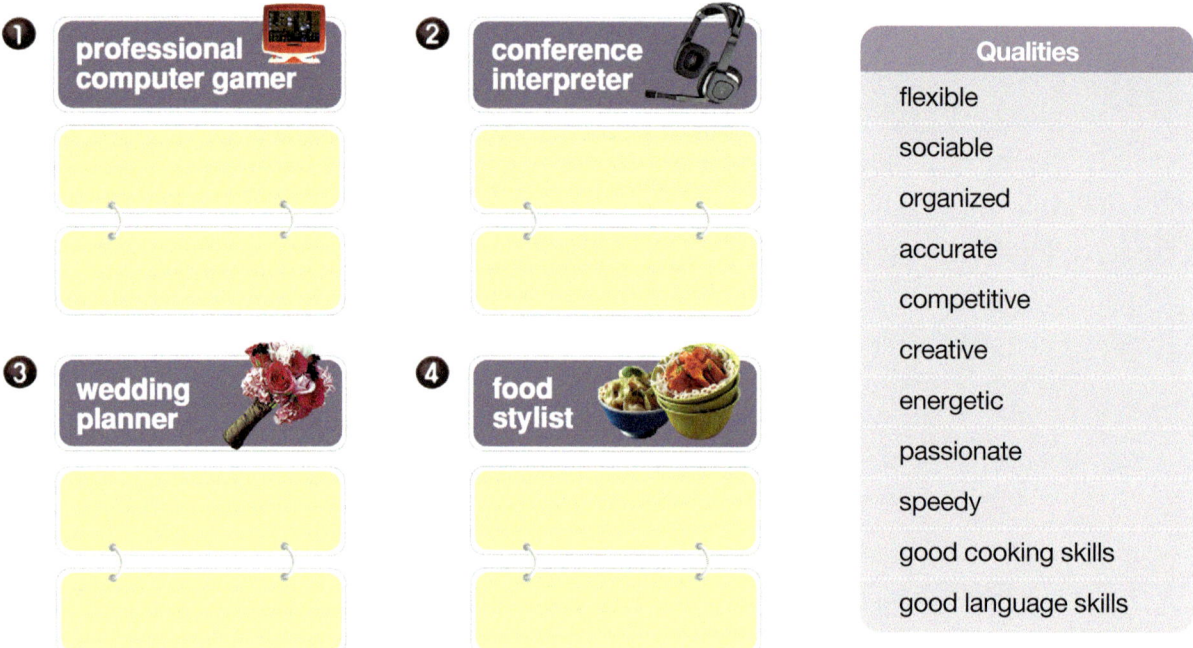

B. Listen to four people talking about their jobs. What qualities are needed for their jobs? What are the things they like about their jobs? Fill in the table below.

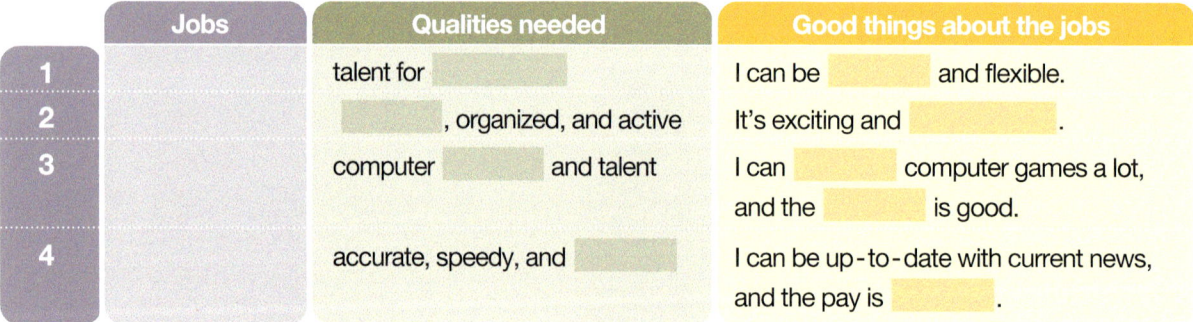

C. With your partner, make up dialogues using the information you got from Part **B**.

> **Example**
>
> **A:** What do you do?
> **B:** I'm a graphic designer.
> **A:** Oh, that's interesting. What qualities are needed for that job?
> **B:** You should have artistic talent and be very patient.
> **A:** What do you like about your job?
> **B:** I get to be very creative. I like designing new things.

Reading

A. These are classified job advertisements in a newspaper. Read the ads and find out what each ad is for.

Wanna Talk

Help wanted

Chefs needed for popular Chinese restaurant
Call now to arrange for interview
2-years experience required
(621) 533-7879

Looking for a Curator

Send your resume to the Department of Arts and Culture at South Western University.
A college degree required.

E-mail: work@uosw.edu.net

Looking for a secretary with a high school diploma.
Computer skills are required.

Contact:
ace21@gmail.com

511-9096

B. Work with a partner. Fill in the conversation below with information from the above job ads. Then role-play your own telephone conversations between job seekers and employers.

Caller: Hello? I saw your ad in the newspaper. Are you still looking for a chef?

Manager: Yes, _____.

Caller: Is it a full-time or part-time position?

Manager: You can work _____.

Caller: What are the working hours?

Manager: You have to work from _____. It starts at _____ and finishes at _____.

Caller: What skills or qualities are needed?

Manager: You need to have _____.

Caller: All right.

Manager: So, if you are interested, send us your resume and we'll give you a call for an interview.

Writing

A. With your partner, talk about your dream jobs with the questions below. Then briefly write down the answers.

1 What is your dream job?

2 What skills or qualities are needed for your dream job?

3 Why is (was) it your dream job?

B. Write a paragraph describing your dream job.

My dream job is to be a pilot. When I was little, I always played with toy airplanes and dreamed of flying my own airplane someday. Now, I'd like to fly a real one. To become a good pilot, I need to be very healthy and have good eyesight. I also need to be trained at a flight training school, and I have to pass an exam. I know it's hard to be a pilot, but I will do my best.

12 Could you ask him to call me back?

Lesson Focus

01 Discussing different modes of communication
02 Using expressions related to making and receiving phone calls
03 Leaving and receiving telephone messages
04 Ways of keeping in touch with people
05 Discussing the advantages and disadvantages of various modes of communication

UNIT 12 Could you ask him to call me back?

Get started

A. There are many different ways to communicate with people. Look at the communication descriptions below and fill in the blanks with the correct methods of communication.

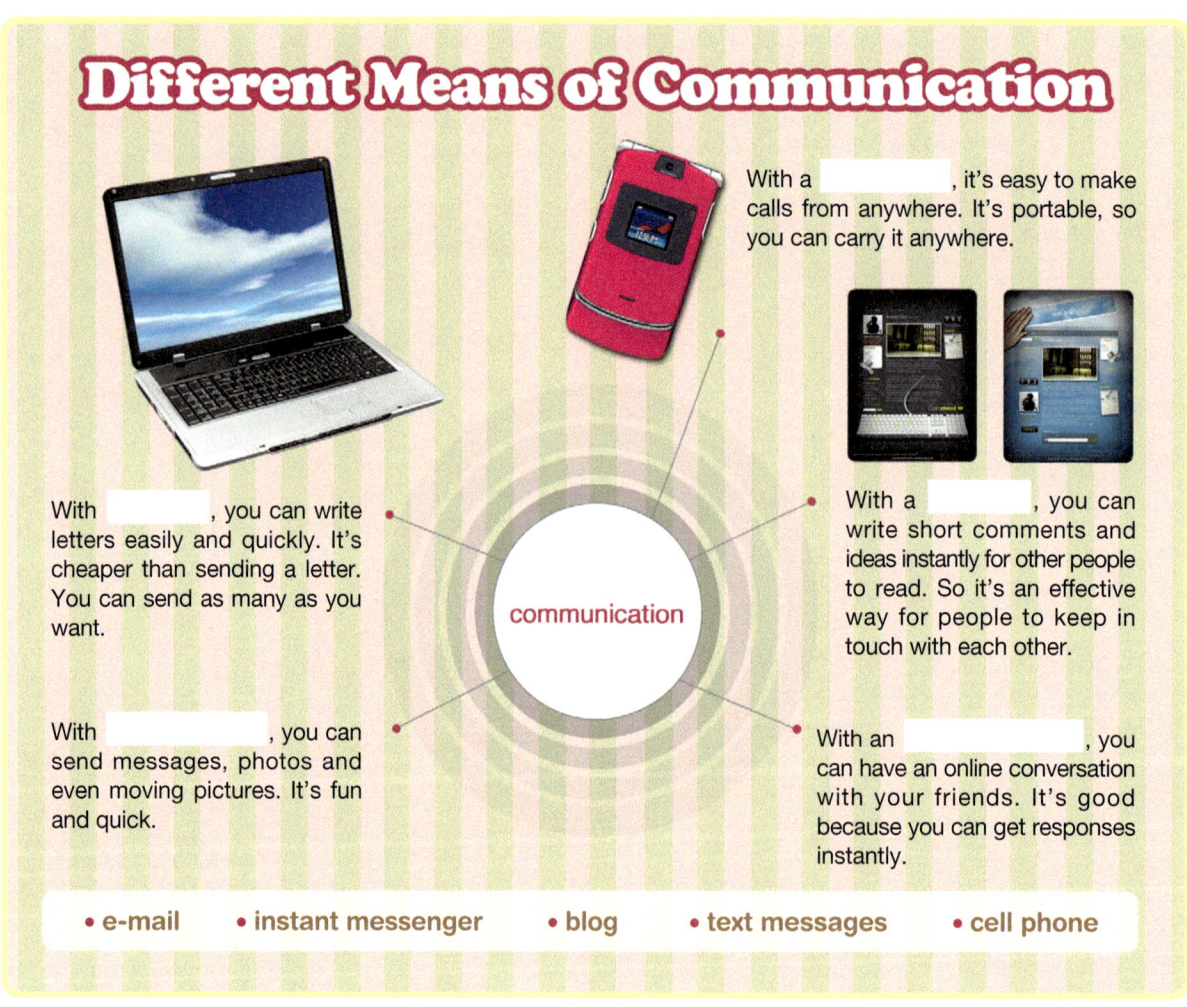

Different Means of Communication

With a _____, it's easy to make calls from anywhere. It's portable, so you can carry it anywhere.

With _____, you can write letters easily and quickly. It's cheaper than sending a letter. You can send as many as you want.

With a _____, you can write short comments and ideas instantly for other people to read. So it's an effective way for people to keep in touch with each other.

With _____, you can send messages, photos and even moving pictures. It's fun and quick.

With an _____, you can have an online conversation with your friends. It's good because you can get responses instantly.

- e-mail
- instant messenger
- blog
- text messages
- cell phone

B. Answer the following questions with your classmates.

1. Which of the above methods of communication do you often use?
2. Do you prefer making calls or sending text messages?
3. Do you ever use an instant messenger? What do you use it for?
4. Do you have your own blog? What do you usually post on it?

Talk together 🎧

Listen to the dialogue and practice.

Sunny: Hello?

Bill: Hello? Is Scott there?

Sunny: I'm sorry, but he is not here right now. He just stepped out, but he'll be back soon. Can you call back later?

Bill: Could you just give him a message for me?

Sunny: Sure. What is it?

Bill: I just wanted to let him know about Shane's birthday party. Please ask him to call me at my place when he gets back.

Sunny: OK. Can I have your phone number?

Bill: It's 554-7946.

Sunny: 554-7946. Is that all?

Bill: Yes, that's all.

Sunny: Okay, I'll tell him to call you back.

Bill: Thank you. Bye.

Sunny: Bye.

Language focus

Caller	Receiver
Can I speak to Scott, please? May I talk to Scott? Is Scott there?	I'm sorry, he's not here right now. He's out to lunch. I'm sorry, he can't answer the phone now. He's at a meeting.
Could you give him a message for me? Can I leave a message?	May I take a message? Would you like to leave a message?
Please ask (tell) him to call me back. Please tell him that Kate called.	OK, I'll give him your message. Does he know your number? Can I have your phone number?

Could you ask him to call me back? • 97

Practice more

A. Complete the dialogue below using the expressions in the *Language Focus* section.

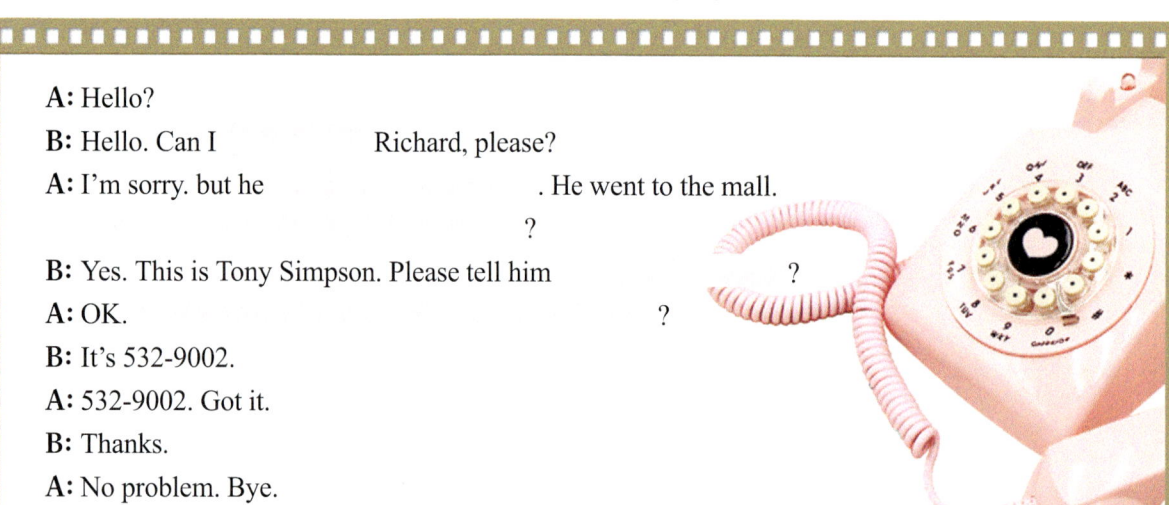

A: Hello?
B: Hello. Can I _____ Richard, please?
A: I'm sorry. but he _____. He went to the mall. _____?
B: Yes. This is Tony Simpson. Please tell him _____?
A: OK. _____?
B: It's 532-9002.
A: 532-9002. Got it.
B: Thanks.
A: No problem. Bye.
B: Bye.

B. Work in pairs. Make up telephone dialogues like the one above using the information below.

- Caller: Susan Smith
- Phone: 670-3702
- Wants to talk to: Dave - in the hospital
  - broke his arm

- Caller: James Morgan
- Phone: 706-2500
- Wants to talk to: Emily - in the library
  - studying for the final exam

- Caller: Fred Miller
- Phone: 986-4178
- Wants to talk to: Nelson - in the yard
  - mowing the lawn

- Caller: Jean Woods
- Phone: 641-1208
- Wants to talk to: Brian - in his room
  - taking a nap

Let's do it 1

A. Daniel just got home and found that he has four phone messages on his answering machine. Listen to the messages and complete the message pads below.

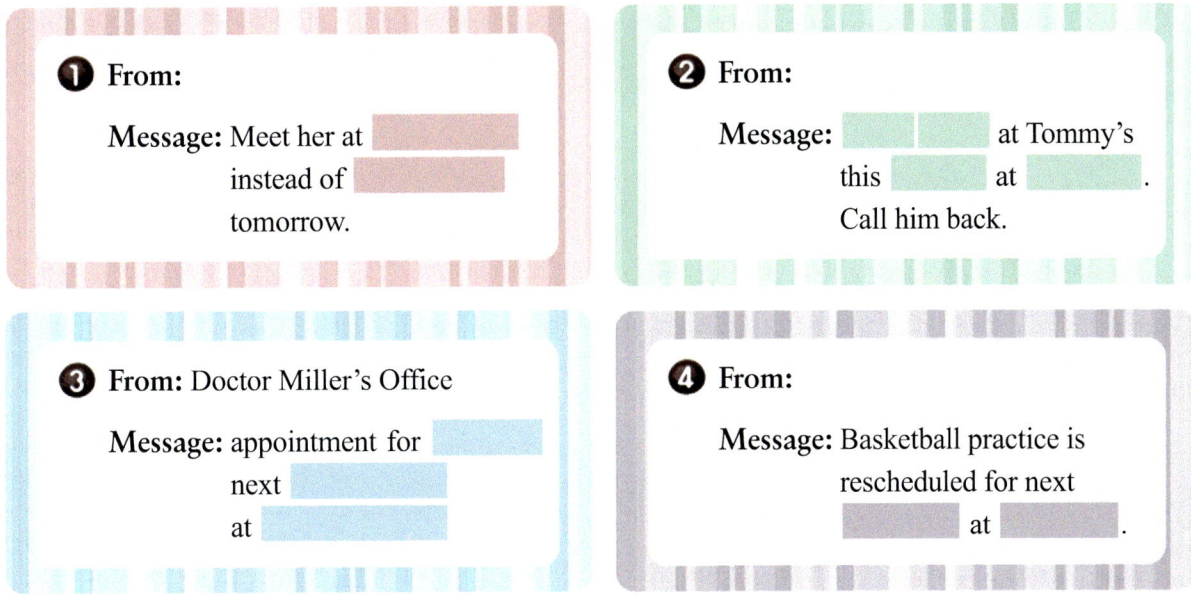

① **From:**

Message: Meet her at _____ instead of _____ tomorrow.

② **From:**

Message: _____ at Tommy's this _____ at _____. Call him back.

③ **From:** Doctor Miller's Office

Message: _____ appointment for next _____ at _____

④ **From:**

Message: Basketball practice is rescheduled for next _____ at _____.

B. Listen again and complete the greeting Daniel recorded on his own answering machine. Then complete the message that Richard left on Daniel's machine.

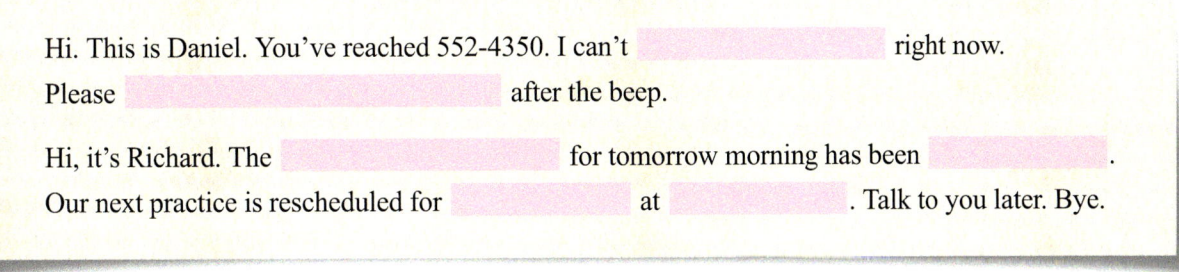

Hi. This is Daniel. You've reached 552-4350. I can't _____ right now. Please _____ after the beep.

Hi, it's Richard. The _____ for tomorrow morning has been _____. Our next practice is rescheduled for _____ at _____. Talk to you later. Bye.

C. Make up your own greeting you would like to record on your own answering machine. You may use the expressions from Daniel's message.

Hi. This is _____. You've reached _____. I can't _____ right now. Please _____. I'll _____.

D. Pretend that you're one of Daniel's friends and want to leave a message on his answering machine. Make up your own message. Refer to the messages above for ideas.

Hi. This is _____.
_____.

Let's do it 2

A. Which methods of communication in the *Get started* section do you often use? Why do you often use those methods? Complete the chart below with your answers.

I often use	Reasons

B. Listen to people talk about the methods of communication they often use and complete the chart by filling in the blanks.

	Methods they often use	Purposes	Reasons
1		To _____ business _____ For ordering and shipping items	_____ and _____
2		To talk to _____ and relatives in other countries	_____ and fast
3		To _____ to and _____ my parents	convenient and _____

C. With your partner, talk about the methods of communication in Part **B**. Use the information in the chart and follow the example below.

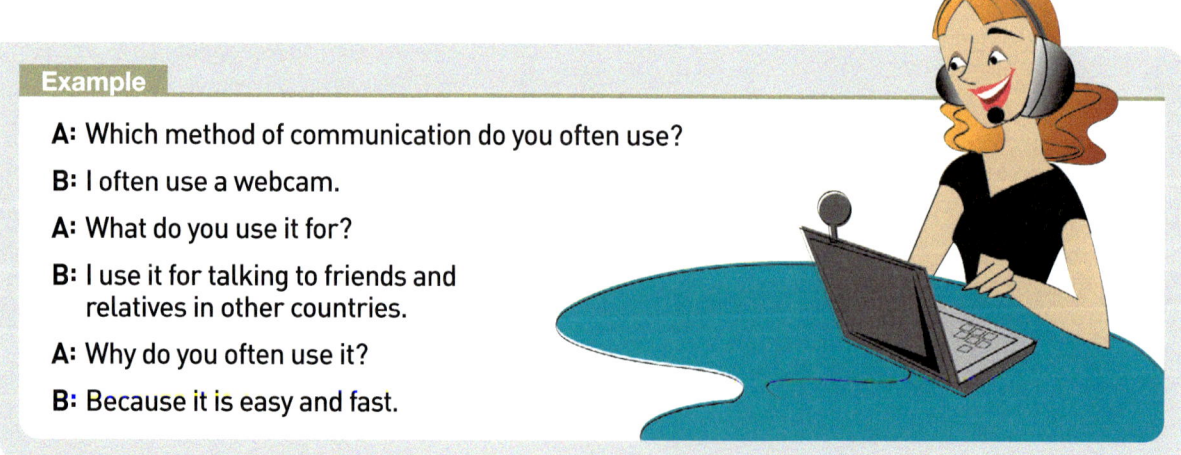

Example

A: Which method of communication do you often use?

B: I often use a webcam.

A: What do you use it for?

B: I use it for talking to friends and relatives in other countries.

A: Why do you often use it?

B: Because it is easy and fast.

Reading

A. Read the passages below about two new methods of communication. Have you ever heard about or used these two methods of communication?

Video conferencing

Video conferencing involves two-way video and audio communication. It is a video link between two or more people who see and hear each other at the same time.

It serves various purposes. It is used for business, education, medical treatments, and security. In an educational setting, video conferencing can be used in schools, libraries, and colleges. By using it, people can meet other people in other locations. People in different countries can have meetings without having to fly abroad. Also, it makes the exchange of information easier and more convenient.

Videophone

A videophone is a telephone that has a video and audio function like videoconferencing. It is different from videoconferencing in that it is for person-to-person communication rather than for groups.

In many science fiction movies and shows about the future, videophones have been used as an important method of communication. In those movies and shows, the main character can be seen communicating with people from other locations. This once sci-fi technology is now becoming a common method of communication.

B. Answer the following questions with your partner.

① Have you ever heard about or used video conferencing?

② What is your opinion of video conferencing?

③ What do people use for it?

④ How could video conferencing be useful to you?

⑤ How about videophones? Have you heard about them before? What do you use them for?

⑥ What is your opinion of videophones?

⑦ How could videophones be useful to you?

Writing

A. Which methods of communication do you use most often? Choose one of the methods from the list. Make a list of words describing the advantages and disadvantages of that method.

- instant messenger
- phone call
- e-mail
- text messaging
- blog

Example

Text messaging	
Advantages	**Disadvantages**
❶ **handy** - you can send and receive messages anytime ❷ **fun** ❸ **cheap** - cheaper than making phone calls	❶ incorrect spellings used ❷ hard to learn ❸ get many spam messages

Advantages	**Disadvantages**

 How are you doing?

Let's do it 1

A. Listen to people introducing each other. They are asking and answering the questions listed below. Complete the answers based on the conversations.

Conversation 1

A: What's your name?
B: I'm Samuel. Just call me Sam.
A: What do you do?
B: I'm a computer programmer.
A: Where do you work?
B: I work for Redman Company.
A: Do you have any brothers or sisters?
B: Yes. I have two sisters and one brother.
A: What do you like to do for fun?
B: I like to travel and take photos.
A: Why do you study English?
B: I study English because I often go on business trips abroad and I also have to speak English at work.

Conversation 2

A: What's your name?
B: I'm Patricia, but you can call me Pat.
A: What do you do?
B: I'm a university student and I study education.
A: What university do you go to?
B: I go to Concord University.
A: Do you have any brothers or sisters?
B: No, I'm an only child.
A: What do you like to do for fun?
B: I enjoy playing the guitar.
A: Why do you study English?
B: Because I want to communicate with people from other countries.

Let's do it 2

A. In the coffee lounge of a trading company, new employees from different departments are talking together. Listen to their conversations and fill in the table.

Conversation 1

Andy: Hello, I think we met at the training session. I'm Andy.
Pam: Oh, you look familiar. I'm Pam.
Andy: I work in the R&D department. I'm a researcher. What do you do?
Pam: I work for the marketing department as a copywriter.
Andy: So, how do you like this company?
Pam: I like the environment. It's bright and cozy. What about you?
Andy: Well, it's nice. I especially like the people here. Anyway, how do you get to work? In my case, I usually take the subway.
Pam: I take the bus. It's very convenient. So, Andy, what do you usually do after work?
Andy: I usually go home and spend time with my family.
Pam: That sounds nice.
Andy: And you? What do you do after work?
Pam: I study Chinese at a language school.
Andy: Wow! You are very diligent.

Conversation 2

Danny: Hello, I'm Danny.
Karen: Oh, hi. I'm Karen.
Danny: Are you new here?
Karen: Yes. I'm a new secretary. And you?
Danny: Me, too. I work in the online business department. I am a web designer. Do you like working here?
Karen: I think so. I mean, the work itself is interesting.
Danny: That's nice.
Karen: What about you? How do you like working here?
Danny: Well, it's not bad. There is a nice atmosphere, and the salary is good.
Karen: I see. So, Danny, how do you get to work?
Danny: I walk. My place is very close-by.
Karen: Really? Good for you. I usually drive, so sometimes the traffic is really bad.
Danny: Do you do anything after work?
Karen: Yes, I go swimming three times a week. What about you?
Danny: I go to a movie or concert once a week.
Karen: Sounds like you enjoy your life.
Danny: Right, I feel refreshed after watching movies or concerts.

 What date is your birthday?

Let's do it 1

A-①. Listen to two dialogues. Fill in the blanks with the correct time.

Conversation 1

A: What time does the library open?
B: It opens at 7 a.m. from Monday to Friday. And on Saturday, it opens at 9 a.m. Why?
A: Well, I have to study for my mid-term exam this week.

I want to be there as early as possible. Then what time does it close?
B: During the weekdays, it closes at 9 p.m. But on Saturday, it closes at 2 p.m.
A: That's great!
I think I'll have enough time to study for my exam.

Conversation 2

A: What are the bank hours?
B: It opens at 9:30 and closes at 5. Why?
A: Because I have to open a new account.
B: Are you going there today?
A: I think so. Why?
B: I'll be going, too.
Shall we go together during the lunch hour?
A: Well, I thought I would go around 4 o'clock, but it's okay for me to go with you.
Maybe we can get a couple sandwiches for lunch.
B: All right.

B-❶. Listen to two dialogues and fill in the blanks with the correct time and dates.

Conversation 1

A: How about going to a movie some time this week?
B: That sounds nice. Which movie did you have in mind?
A: Miss Potter.
B: Great. What day would you like to go?
A: There are three showings in the morning on Saturday. How about the first showing?
B: What time does it start?
A: It starts at 10:40 a.m.
B: By the way, what date is this Saturday?
A: It's the 12th.
B: All right. Where shall we meet?
A: Let's meet in front of the Grand Bookstore at 10:30.
B: Okay. I'll see you then.

Conversation 2

A: Would you like to see a musical this Wednesday?
B: That would be nice. Is this Wednesday the 8th?
A: Right.
B: So which musical is it?
A: "Only You". Have you ever seen it?
B: No. Have you?
A: Yes, it's fantastic. And I really want to see it again.
B: What is it about?
A: Well, I don't want to tell you the whole story, but I can guarantee that you will enjoy this romantic and touching musical.
B: All right. So, what time does it start?
A: It starts at 7:30 and finishes at 9.
Do you think you can make it?
B: Of course.

Let's do it 2

A. Listen to Rachel's plans for February. Fill in the blanks in the calendar with the correct event.

In February, I have a number of plans, events and appointments to attend. February the 8th is my birthday. I am going to eat out at a Chinese restaurant with my family at 7 p.m. On Monday the 12th, I have to see my dentist at 10 a.m. On the 14th, it's Valentine's Day. I'm going to see a movie with my boyfriend at 7:30 p.m. Then on Wednesday the 21st I have to go to my high school reunion at the Sheraton Hotel. It starts at 6:30 p.m. And on the 25th, I am going to my best friend Anna's wedding. I am really excited about seeing my friend in a beautiful wedding gown. The wedding starts at 1:00 p.m.

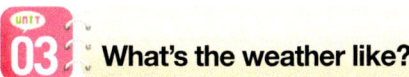

What's the weather like?

Practice more

A. Listen to people talking about the weather. Match the pictures with the proper descriptions.

Ⓐ It's freezing and windy. It's 5 degrees below zero Celsius.
Ⓑ It's hot and humid. It's 30 degrees Celsius.
Ⓒ It's sunny and warm. The temperature is 70 degrees Fahrenheit.
Ⓓ It's cold and rainy. The temperature is 45 degrees Fahrenheit.

Let's do it 1

A. Listen to today's weather forecasts for a number of cities around the world. Fill out the chart below with the information you hear.

Good news, folks! It will be another warm day here in San Francisco. We'll be enjoying sunny skies all day long. Temperatures will reach around 57 degrees Fahrenheit.

Take your umbrella to work today! Paris will be mostly rainy today with a high of around 13 degrees Celsius. Winds will make temperatures feel cooler.

Partly cloudy skies are expected for Auckland this morning. However, a 40% chance of rain is expected for the afternoon. Temperatures will reach 21 degrees Celsius.

And now for the weather. Hong Kong will be hot and muggy. The temperature will likely reach as high as 28 degrees Celsius by noon. Mostly clear skies are also in the forecast.

In Toronto, there will be a few showers early in the morning. Temperatures will cool off toward the afternoon. Lows will drop to around 9 degrees Celsius.

Let's do it 2

A. Listen to four people talking about their favorite seasons. Fill in the table below based on what you hear.

Ⓐ My name is Olivia. I live in Auckland. My favorite season is summer. It's hot and sunny. It also rains a lot during the summer. I love doing summer sports, such as swimming, windsurfing, and scuba diving. But I don't like reading books, listening to music or staying at home.

Ⓑ I'm Matt and I'm from Vancouver. Winter is the best season here. It can get quite cold and windy, and the mountains get covered in snow. Of course, my favorite sport is skiing. There are many nice ski resorts near my city. I also like snowboarding. We have nice hiking trails as well, but I don't think it's a good idea to go hiking in winter.

Ⓒ I'm Angela from Glasgow, Scotland. We have the most beautiful spring in the world, and it's my favorite season. It's still chilly outside, but when the skies are clear, we have beautiful, sunny days. It's very good to go hiking in the mountains because you can see many beautiful flowers. And especially like going fishing with my dad. I don't like cycling because that requires a lot of energy. It's better to go for a walk in the spring.

Ⓓ My name is Joel and I live in Tokyo. I love all seasons in Tokyo, but I like autumn the best because the weather is cool and windy. However, sometimes it's humid. Going on a picnic is a very good way to enjoy nature outside of Tokyo. I love going camping or going for a drive in the countryside. The weather is good for outdoor activities, but I don't like riding a bike or walking in the city because of the air pollution.

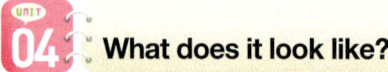

What does it look like?

Let's do it 1

A. Listen to the descriptions of the items in the picture. Put the number of the description on the correct picture.

❶ It is red and has a small light bulb in it. It is used for lighting dark places.

❷ It is made of plastic. It has water in it. It comes in many different shapes. It is used for adding moisture to the air.

❸ It is round and has numbers on it. It is used for telling the time and it helps you get up in the morning.

❹ It is long and made of wood. It has cloth at the end of it. It is used for cleaning the floor.

❺ It is brown, rectangular, and has a long strap. It is made of leather. It is used for carrying a laptop computer.

❻ It is long and pointy. It has a handle. It is used to protect you against the rain or snow.

Let's do it 2

B. People are talking about buying one of the two items above. Listen to the conversations and fill in the table.

Conversation 1

Michael: Sally, I heard you were going to buy a PDA.
Sally: Well, I'm still thinking about it.
Michael: Why?
Sally: Actually I'm not sure what the differences are between a personal planner and a PDA.
Michael: Well, there are many differences. First of all, a PDA is more convenient than a personal planner because it holds a lot more information. It is also easier to search for information with a PDA. A PDA can also store large electronic files and documents, so you don't have to carry hard-copies of all your files.
Sally: In that case, I will definitely buy a PDA! Thanks a lot.

Conversation 2

Daniel: Julie, I'm not sure which one I should buy- a desktop computer or a laptop.
Julie: What are you going to use the computer for mainly?
Daniel: To search for information on the web, write reports and give presentations at meetings.
Julie: And you go on a lot of business trips, don't you?
Daniel: That's right.
Julie: Then you may want to buy a laptop computer because it's more handy to carry around. The price has gone down a lot, so it's not as expensive as it used to be. You can check out Gadget Plaza on Broadway. They have laptops on sale now.
Daniel: Great! I'm going to go there right now.

Conversation 3

Craig: Hey, Brian! I need your advice on buying a car.
Brian: OK. What kind of a car would you like to buy?
Craig: Maybe a mid-sized sedan or an SUV. I can't make up my mind.
Brian: I'd recommend an SUV because it's more practical. I mean, you can carry a lot of stuff when you travel or when you need to move large items.
Craig: But SUVs are more expensive than sedans. I am on a tight budget.
Brian: How about buying a used one? One of my friends is a used car dealer.
I think he can give you a good deal.
Craig: Oh, really? That would be great!
Brian: I'll tell him to get in touch with you.

UNIT 05 Do you have any plans for the weekend?

Let's do it 1

A. Imagine that you live in San Francisco and want to attend some events that are going to take place in March. So you'd like to find out information about what kinds of events are going to be held. Listen to the part of the radio show that informs you of some of the events not listed on the calendar below. Then write the number of the events on the correct dates.

A: So, are there any cultural events worth going to?
B: Yeah, there are. I was thinking of going to one of them.
A: Can you recommend one in particular?
B: There is going to be a magic show on March 1st.
A: Interesting. Where is that taking place?
B: At Berkeley Theatre. There is also a flea market opening on March 4th at Golden Gate Park.
A: I'm definitely going to check that out. How about art shows?
B: Oh yeah, there is a Japanese print exhibit at the San Francisco Museum of Modern Art on the 22nd.
A: I'm not familiar with Japanese art, but I'd like to go see the exhibition.
B: I think it would be worth seeing. And one more thing. You might like this one. The Hilton Hotel plans to offer a Sunday brunch special on the 25th to celebrate their anniversary. It will be only $10.00 per person.
A: Sounds great. I really enjoy going out for brunch on Sundays. Would you like to go together?
B: Sure.

Let's do it 2

B. Listen to people talking about their future hopes and plans. Check if the following statements are True or False. Then check the answers with your partner.

Conversation 1

Amanda: Hey, it's almost New Year's Day. Have you made your resolutions?
Bob: I haven't thought about them much. How about you?
Amanda: Yeah. I'm planning to go on a diet. I have put on a few pounds since the summer.
Bob: Good for you. Hmm... I have always wanted to try scuba diving. That might be worth trying for the new year. I might also try rock climbing. I have heard that it is pretty fun.
Amanda: Cool! I would be interested in trying rock climbing, too. Do you want to look into lessons together?
Bob: That would be awesome!

Conversation 2

Katherine: Can you imagine where we will be in five years from now?
Elizabeth: Five years from now? Man, that seems so far off, but I think time is going to fly.
Katherine: I agree. I hope to be settled in a good job and own my own home at that point.
Elizabeth: You are a hard-working person. I'm sure you will achieve those goals. I personally hope to be married and have kids within the next five years or so.
Katherine: Really? I thought you wanted to become a nurse. You are, after all, in nursing school.
Elizabeth: Right. By the time I am five years older, I will be able to balance both my family and my career.
Katherine: I am sure you will.

Conversation 3

Liz: Have you thought much about your retirement?
Eric: Not really. How about you?
Liz: Well, I don't want to end up with nothing to do in my old age.
Eric: I agree. I'd like to take up golfing when I retire. It is a great way to enjoy the outdoors and get some exercise. I have also always been interested in painting. It would give me something to do when I'm older.
Liz: That sounds like a good plan. Actually, I have always really enjoyed sailing. If I have enough money by the time I retire, I'd like to buy a small yacht to cruise around in.
Eric: That would be lovely.

UNIT 06 What kind of dress are you looking for?

Let's do it 1

A. There's a big year-end sale going on at Oak Valley Shopping Mall. Listen to the conversations and write down what the people are going to buy. Then referring to the pictures below, write the type of store they will buy each item from.

Conversation 1

Salesperson: Can I help with anything?
Customer: Yes, I'm looking for a pair of rollerblades.
Salesperson: Is there a particular style you're looking for?
Customer: I'd like a pair with a metal frame. And I prefer rather dark colors.
Salesperson: How about these navy ones? You can try these on.
Customer: They fit perfectly. What's the price? I saw that these are on sale.
Salesperson: That's right. They were originally $80.00, but with a 20% discount, they come to $64.00 plus tax.
Customer: That's quite reasonable.
Salesperson: If you buy these, we give a second pair of rollerblades for half price.
Customer: That's a great idea! I'll buy these.

Listening Script • 107

Conversation 2

Salesperson: May I help you?
Customer: I'm interested in looking at some down-filled pillows?
Salesperson: We carry a number of different kinds. Take a look.
Customer: They look good. Do you have any goose down pillows?
Salesperson: Sure. They are right over here.
Customer: Do they come in a flowered pattern?
Salesperson: Yes, they do. How about these?
Customer: Oh, lovely. I'll buy these ones. How much are they?
Salesperson: The price tag says $50.00, but they are on sale now. So you can get a 50 % discount. The final price will be $25.00 each.
Customer: Oh, that is a great deal. I am glad that I stopped in here today.

Conversation 3

Salesperson: Good afternoon. Can I help you?
Customer: I need to buy a digital camcorder.
Salesperson: You came to the right place. We sell a variety of digital camcorders and we are actually having a 20% off sale right now on all camcorders.
Customer: Great. I'm looking for a camcorder with a quality zoom lens.
Salesperson: How about this one?
Customer: Hmmm, this one has a good zoom lens, but I want a camcorder with a wider screen.
Salesperson: How about this one?
Customer: Oh, I like this one. How much is it?
Salesperson: With the 20% discount, it is $475.00.
Customer: I'll take it.

Conversation 4

Salesperson: Good morning. Can I help you?
Customer: Yes, I'm looking for a carry-on bag.
Salesperson: What kind of bag did you have in mind?
Customer: Well, it should be rather small. I need to be able to carry it when I fly.
Salesperson: Fortunately, we have a number of small, light-weight carry-ons in stock. What do you think of this one?
Customer: Umm, it's the right size but I don't like the green color.
Salesperson: No problem. This line also comes in black, gray, red, and blue.
Customer: Actually the red one would be nice. How much is it?
Salesperson: As a matter of fact, it was $200.00 until yesterday. They are now 30% off. Your timing was perfect!
Customer: So it will be only $140.00. Great! I'll take it.

Let's do it 2

B. Listen to the conversations between sales representatives and customers. Write down the problems with each and check(✓) how the problems were taken care of.

Conversation 1

Operator: CVS online shopping. How may I help you?
Customer: Hi, I bought a jacket online a few days ago and I'd like to exchange it for another one.
Operator: May I ask what the problem is?
Customer: I think the zipper was broken during the delivery.
Operator: Oh, we're terribly sorry. Please send it back to us and we will deliver you a new one.
Customer: Thanks for the help.
Operator: You're welcome.

Conversation 2

Operator: Cell Factory. How can I help you?
Customer: Hi, I purchased this cell phone through your online shopping site and received it a week ago.
Operator: Is there a problem with it?
Customer: Yes, the battery dies too quickly. It lasts for only a few hours. So can I get a refund for this?
Operator: I'm sorry, but we don't give refunds for used cell phones.
Customer: Then what should I do about this?
Operator: We can send you a new battery. If that doesn't work, you will need to stop by our local service center.
Customer: I see. Thanks.

Conversation 3

Operator: Steven's Shoes. How may I help you?
Customer: Hi, I bought a pair of shoes through your catalogue, and I found something wrong with them?
Operator: What is wrong with them?
Customer: The ribbon on one of the shoes came off as soon as I put them on.
Operator: Oh, it must have been poorly attached. I'm sorry about that. We will give you a full refund. We're going to cancel your credit card payment right away. And we'll send a delivery person to collect the shoes.
Customer: OK. Thanks a lot.

Conversation 4

Operator: Urban Outfitters. What can I do for you?
Customer: Hi, I bought a skirt the other day, online. There's a problem.
Operator: Can you tell me what's wrong with it?
Customer: Yes, it's just too big for me. It's the wrong size. Can I get a refund for this?
Operator: I'm sorry, but we don't give refunds for clothes.
Customer: Then can you exchange it for a smaller size?

Operator: That's possible. What was the size that you wanted to order?
Customer: Size six, please.
Operator: Okay. Please send your skirt back to us and we will send you a new one in size six.
Customer: Thank you.

Unit 07 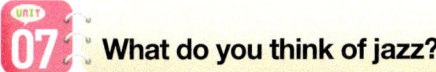 What do you think of jazz?

Let's do it 1

B. A reporter at the university monthly newspaper plans to write an article about the students' likes and dislikes related to entertainment. Listen to him interviewing three students. Fill in the chart below with the kinds of entertainment the three students like.

Reporter: Thanks for speaking with me today, guys. So, let's get started. First of all, Grace, do you enjoy listening to music?
Grace: Yeah, I like it a lot, actually.
Reporter: Great. And what kind of music do you like listening to?
Grace: Mostly pop music. And dance is pretty good, too.
Reporter: How about you, Richard?
Richard: Actually I really like rock music. I especially like listening to rock when I am driving.
Reporter: Oh, I see. And Tracy? Do you like rock music, too?
Tracy: As a matter of fact, I hate it, but I love jazz. No offence, Richard.
Richard: None taken.
Reporter: Okay, now let's talk about sports. Richard, do you like sports?
Richard: Yes, very much.
Reporter: What kinds of sports do you like to play?
Richard: I like soccer, mostly. But I also like hockey.
Reporter: And you, Grace? Do you like sports?
Grace: I really like playing tennis, I usually play on Sundays.
Reporter: Good for you. How about you, Tracy? Do you like tennis as well?
Tracy: Yeah, it's okay. But I'm crazy about golf. It is my dream to become a professional golfer one day.
Reporter: That would be nice. Okay, now for the last question. What kinds of movies do you like, uh... Grace?
Grace: I like horror movies.
Reporter: And Richard? What do you think of horror movies?
Richard: I don't really like horror movies. I prefer science fiction.
Reporter: Interesting. How about you, Tracy?
Tracy: Uh, comedies, especially romantic comedies, are my favorite.

Reporter: Well, thank you very much for your time, everyone. I really appreciate it.

Let's do it 2

A. People are talking about their favorite pastimes while looking at information about events that will be held this weekend. Listen to the conversations and put the number of the conversation in the correct box.

Conversation 1

A: Do you like watching soccer games?
B: Yes, of course. I'm surprised that you didn't know I like watching soccer. And my favorite soccer player is Ronaldo.
A: Really? I'm a big fan of his, too. I've got two free tickets for the soccer tournament. Do you want to go?
B: Are you sure?
A: Yes, why would I lie to you? It's this Saturday at 7:30. Can you make it?
B: Absolutely.
A: Okay, then I'll see you at the stadium at 6:50. There'll be a lot of traffic so I recommend taking the subway.
B: All right. I'll see you there. Bye.

Conversation 2

A: Do you have any special plans for this weekend?
B: No, not really. Why?
A: If you like, we could go to watch the musical "The Lion King"
B: That's a good idea. I didn't know that you like watching musicals in your free time.
A: Yes. What about you?
B: I do too, actually. I like it. What's your favorite musical?
A: Well, there are so many of them. But "Mamma Mia" is probably my favorite.
B: Really? Same as me. I especially like its lively songs and dancing.
A: I agree. So, it's this Saturday at 5 o'clock and admission is $35.00 for an adult. Is that okay with you?
B: Okay.

Conversation 3

A: What do you like to do in your free time?
B: I like to go to concerts. What about you? How do you like going to concerts?
A: I love it. What kind of concerts do you like?
B: I like pop concerts.
A: Oh, I like them a lot, too. The pop groups, Little Princess is performing this weekend. Would you like to go this Saturday?
B: Sure. Let me check the time and the ticket price. Hmm. I think I can make it.

Conversation 4

A: What are your favorite free time activities?
B: Umm, I like reading novels, watching movies and doing outdoor activities.

A: Don't you like watching plays?
B: I like them, too, but the thing is that I haven't seen many of them.
A: Would you like to see one? It's Shakespeare's play, "Hamlet".
B: Wow! Wonderful! I've read it, but I've never seen it on stage.
A: You'll like it. It's this Sunday at 7:30.
B: Okay, let's go. Can we buy the tickets in advance?
A: Why not? They're $10.00 for students. I guess that's quite cheap. I'll buy the tickets and you can pay me later.
B: All right.

Conversation 5

A: What do you like to do in your free time?
B: I like to go jazz dancing.
A: Interesting. How long have you been doing that?
B: Well, only a few months. I first started to learn it as an exercise. It's so much fun.
A: Really? It looks like you really enjoy doing it.
B: Yes, I think so.
A: Then would you like to go to a dance festival together this Friday.
B: What kinds of dances are they showing?
A: There are jazz, pop, salsa, techno and many more.
B: That's wonderful!

UNIT 08 What would you like to have?

Let's do it 1

A. Lisa and Brandon are ordering their lunch at a restaurant. Listen to the conversation and check the food they ordered from the menu. Then write down the food in the table below.

W: May I take your order?
L: Yes, I'd like the pork tenderloin, please.
B: I'll have grilled chicken wings.
W: All right. Would you like an appetizer first?
L: OK. I'll have clam chowder and garlic bread.
B: I'd like fried calamari.
W: Would you like soup or salad?
L: I'll have the garden salad.
B: I'd like the potato and onion soup.
W: What kind of dressing would you like with your salad?
L: French dressing, please.
W: Would you care for something to drink?
B: A glass of lemon iced tea for me, please.
L: Me, too.
W: Anything for dessert?
L&B: No, thank you.

Let's do it 2

A. Listen to the recipe of a dish and complete the ingredients list. Then complete the procedures by filling in the blanks based on what you hear.

Ⓐ Making egg fried rice with shrimp is not hard. Here is an easy recipe. First, you fry onions, carrots, and peas together for five minutes. Then you stir the shrimp with the other ingredients and fry it for another two minutes. Next, you beat two eggs and pour them into the mixture. Cook it for three minutes, then add the cooked rice. Finally, pour in a little soy sauce and serve. It only takes about 10 minutes to make.

Ⓑ These pictures show how to make an omelet, but they are not in order. Listen to the recipe and number the pictures in the correct order from 1 to 6.

① First, break some eggs into a bowl. And whisk the eggs with the salt and pepper.

② Next beat in the milk, parsley, and cheese.

③ Then heat some oil in a pan. Olive oil is best, but you can use ordinary corn oil if you want. You should not let the oil get too hot.

④ Pour the egg mixture into the pan, and spread it evenly. Fry a little.

⑤ When the egg mixture gets a little hard, fold it in half.

⑥ After a couple of minutes, turn the omelet over. Be careful not to break it. When the omelet is cooked, serve it immediately. It tastes best when it's hot.

UNIT 09 Are you under the weather?

Let's do it 1

A-2. Listen to the conversations. Put the number of the conversation on the correct picture.

Conversation 1

Pharmacist: Hello. What can I do for you?
Robert: Hello, I have a prescription from a doctor. I have the flu.
Pharmacist: Okay, let me get that for you. (a few seconds later) OK. Here you are. You should take two pills every six hours, and take one spoonful of this syrup before each meal. You may also want to get plenty of rest.
Robert: Okay. Thanks.

Conversation 2

Louise: Hi, Clint. This is Louise. How are you today?
Clint: I don't feel good. I have a sore throat.
Louise: I'm sorry to hear that.
Clint: I don't have time to go to see a doctor. Could you recommend a home remedy?
Louise: You may want to gargle with salt water? And

you should keep drinking lots of warm water.
Clint: Thanks. Those are good ideas.

Conversation 3

Doctor: What seems to be the problem?
Patient: While I was playing football yesterday, I twisted my ankle. It's killing me.
Doctor: Hmm... Let me see. You will have to keep your leg in a cast for a month.
Patient: Oh, my goodness. I am supposed to play in the final match in two weeks!

Conversation 4

Doctor: What seems to be the matter?
Patient: I burnt my finger while I was cooking last night. I put some ice on it, but it still hurts a lot.
Doctor: Let me take a look. It's not that bad. Put this ointment on it. Also, avoid getting any water on the burnt finger.
Patient: OK. I see.

Let's do it 2

B. Listen to the conversations between a receptionist and a patient. What's wrong with each patient? Which doctor should they see? Write the number of the conversation on the correct picture.

Conversation 1

Receptionist: Hello, this is St. Mary's hospital. What can I do for you?
Lara: I think I need to see a dermatologist. I have pimples all over my face.
Receptionist: Is that all?
Lara: Yes. What time can I come in?
Receptionist: Well, I can put you on the list for 3:00 p.m. tomorrow.

Conversation 2

Receptionist: Hello, this is Dr. Smith's office. May I help you?
Nick: Hello, can I see the doctor as soon as possible?
Receptionist: May I ask what is wrong?
Nick: When I was playing football this morning and I think I sprained my wrist. It's killing me.
Receptionist: I think you have called the wrong doctor's office. Dr. Smith is an optometrist.
Nick: Oh, I'm sorry. Can you recommend another doctor who can have a look at my wrist?
Receptionist: Sure, Dr. Lee next door can probably see you right away.

Conversation 3

Receptionist: Good morning. Can I help you?
Vicky: Hi, I'm not feeling well and I'd like to make an appointment with a doctor, but I don't know who I should see.
Receptionist: What are your symptoms?
Vicky: I have a headache and my nose is runny. I also keep sneezing. I think I have a fever as well.
Receptionist: You'd better see Dr. Williams - she's one of our physicians. When would you like to make an appointment for?

Conversation 4

Receptionist: Hello. How can I help you?
Monica: Hello, I have a terrible toothache.
Receptionist: When was your last checkup?
Monica: Well... I can't remember... but I think it was more than a year ago.
Receptionist: Hmmm... you may have a cavity. Unfortunately, Dr. Kim is booked all week. The earliest he can see you is next Monday.
Monica: I think I can come in Monday morning.
Receptionist: Great. I'll give you a 10 o'clock appointment.

UNIT 10 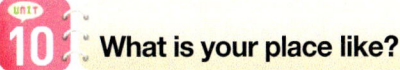 What is your place like?

Let's do it 1

A. Listen to people talking about their places. Fill in the table based on the conversations.

Conversation 1

Leo: Hi, Dora. How do you like your new apartment?
Dora: I like it a lot.
Leo: Where is it located?
Dora: It's near St. James's park.
Leo: What is the apartment like?
Dora: It has six rooms: two bedrooms, two bathrooms, a kitchen, and a living room.
Leo: Sounds great. What do you like about it?
Dora: It has a nice laundry room and a well-equipped gym.
Leo: Wow, is there a swimming pool, too?
Dora: Yeah. Actually, there are two swimming pools.

Conversation 2

Peter: Are you all settled in?
Tracy: Almost. Thanks for asking.
Peter: So, what is your apartment like?
Tracy: It's a studio apartment with a separate kitchen.
Peter: Where is it located?
Tracy: It is in the Bloomingdale area, near my work.
Peter: Oh, good for you. So what do you like about your apartment?
Tracy: It's very cozy with good interior design. And there is a big swimming pool and a jacuzzi.
Peter: It sounds like it's perfect for you. Invite me over sometime so I can take a look.
Tracy: Sure. I'll have a housewarming party soon.

Conversation 3

Jack: Honey, can you remember our old house?
Kate: Which house are you talking about? Where was it located?
Jack: It was near the river.
Kate: What was it like? I can't remember exactly.
Jack: It had three large bedrooms and a big kitchen. You really liked the kitchen.
Kate: Right! We spent a few good years there with the children.
Jack: Yeah. I sometimes miss the nice river view.
Kate: There was quite a big garden, too. We enjoyed many Sunday barbecues there.

Let's do it 2

A. Tenants and landlords are talking on the phone about the problems in the tenants' apartments. Listen to the conversations and number the pictures.

Conversation 1

Mr. Peterson: Hello, this is the Peterson's residence.
George: Hello, Mr. Peterson. This is George on King Road.
Mr. Peterson: Hello, George. You don't sound happy. Let me guess. Something went wrong with your house.
George: Yeah, right. The lights in the hallway are not working. When I got home last night, I almost fell down. I had to light a candle to find my way.
Mr. Peterson: Oh, my goodness. It is not easy to repair the electricity in that house.
George: Isn't it?
Mr. Peterson: Anyway, I'll get an electrician to have a look.
George: How soon will that be?
Mr. Peterson: Within a few hours.
George: Good. Thank you.

Conversation 2

Mr. Smith: Hello?
Peter: Is this Mr. Smith?
Mr. Smith: Yes, speaking.
Peter: Hi, Mr. Smith. It's Peter Walsh, your tenant in apartment 2B.
Mr. Smith: Hi, Mr. Walsh. What's the matter?
Peter: I'm calling because the heater stopped working. I woke up this morning and the house was freezing. My wife and I have a terrible cold now.
Mr. Smith: Oh, I'm sorry to hear that. I'll send the repairperson over.
Peter: Will that be today?
Mr. Smith: Yes, of course. It will be sometime before noon.
Peter: Great. Thank you so much.

Conversation 3

Nora: Hello, can I speak to Mrs. Jackson?
Mrs. Jackson: This is Mrs. Jackson. Who's speaking, please?
Nora: Oh, hi. This is Nora.
Mrs. Jackson: Hi, Nora. How are you doing?
Nora: Well, actually there is a big problem with the toilet. It overflowed this morning. There's water everywhere. I don't know what to do.
Mrs. Jackson: Good heavens. You need a plumber. I'll sort it out right now.
Nora: Okay. Thank you.
Mrs. Jackson: You're welcome. Call me anytime if there is anything else that needs to be repaired.
Nora: OK. Thank you.
Mrs. Jackson: My pleasure.

UNIT 11 Who does he work for?

Let's do it 1

B. Listen to the Conversations and fill out the chart.

Conversation 1

A: What do you do?
B: I am a college student. I go to Thomson College.
A: What do you study?
B: I study architecture.
A: What exactly do you learn?
B: Basically, I learn about designing buildings and structures.
A: How do you like your major?
B: I like it very much. It's always exciting for me because I like building things.

Conversation 2

A: What do you do?
B: I am a florist.
A: Who do you work for?
B: I run my own flower shop.
A: What exactly do you do at work?
B: I arrange flowers for customers.
A: What do you think of your job?
B: It's very rewarding because I'm happy to see people smile when I arrange flowers for them.

Conversation 3

A: What do you do?
B: I'm a bank teller.
A: Who do you work for?
B: I work at Ace Bank.
A: What exactly do you do at work?
B: I provide customers with information about their accounts and banking services.
A: What do you think of your job?
B: Sometimes it's stressful because you always have to be friendly when interacting with customers.

Conversation 4

A: What do you do?
B: I'm a party planner.
A: Who do you work for?
B: I am a freelancer.
A: What exactly do you do at work?
B: I make arrangements for party locations, food and decorations.
A: What do you think of your job?
B: It's very fun because I can be creative.

Let's do it 2

B. Listen to four people talking about their jobs. What qualities are needed for their jobs? What are the things they like about their jobs? Fill in the table below.

❶

I'm Erin Johnson. I am a food stylist. To become a food stylist, you should begin with a strong will and talent for cooking. I really enjoy working as a food stylist. I can be creative and flexible by cooking and styling many kinds of dishes.

❷

I'm Catherine Fonda and I work as a wedding planner. It's a very exciting and rewarding job. To become a wedding planner, you don't have to have any special education or experience. But you need to be sociable, organized, and active because you have to deal with many demanding customers. I like this job because it's rewarding to see people enjoy beautiful weddings.

❸

My name is Jonathan Rogers. I am a professional computer gamer. I play computer games at tournaments for prize money. I am energetic and passionate. To become a professional computer gamer, you need to have great computer skills and talent. The good things about this job are that I get paid well and I can play computer games as much as I want.

❹

My name is Adriana Taylor. After graduating from a translation school, I got a job working as a conference interpreter. I love this job. It's exciting and interesting. To be a good interpreter, you need to be accurate, speedy, and flexible. I think my personality and this job match very well. I also like this job because I can always keep up-to-date with the current news. I am also paid well.

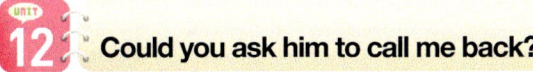

Unit 12: Could you ask him to call me back?

Let's do it 1

A. Daniel just got home and found that he has four phone messages on his answering machine. Listen to the messages and complete the message pads below.

(answering machine) Hi. This is Daniel. You've reached 552-4350. I can't answer the phone right now. Please leave me a message after the beep. (beep~~)

❶ Hi, Daniel. It's Kate. About our plans tomorrow, I get off from work a little earlier. So let's meet at 6 instead of 6:30. So I'll see you then. Bye.

❷ Hey, Daniel. This is Wilson. How are you doing? How about having dinner together at Tommy's this Saturday at 7:30. Is it okay with you? There's something I need to talk to you about. Give me a call later.

❸ Hello. This is Dr. Miller's Office. You have an appointment at 10 a.m. on Monday, next week. Please make sure you make it to your eye appointment.

❹ Hi, it's Richard. Daniel, the basketball practice for tomorrow morning has been cancelled. Our next practice is rescheduled for next Saturday, the 15th, at 9 in the morning. Talk to you later. Bye.

Let's do it 2

B. Listen to people talk about the methods of communication they often use and complete the chart by filling in the blanks.

❶ I often use e-mail to communicate with other people. I work at a trading company, so I use e-mail to write business letters and for ordering and shipping items. I like using e-mail because it's quick and convenient.

❷ In my case, I often use an instant messenger. I use it to talk to my friends and relatives who live far away in other countries. It's easy to use because all you have to do is just log into the messenger program, and write messages. It's very fast. When you send messages to other people, you get a reply right away.

❸ Webcams make my life more enjoyable. I live in the school dormitory, so I miss my family a lot. But with a web cam, I can see my parents in person on the monitor and they can also see me. We can talk and see each other at the same time. It's very convenient and economical. I don't have to travel far to see my parents if I have my computer equipped with a web cam and a connection to the Internet.

Wanna Talk
An integrated course for communicative success